DATE DUE

02	08	002	
OCT 15 2002			
GAYLORD			PRINTED IN U.S.A.

In memory of

J. J. Reneaux
December 11, 1955–February 29, 2000

Richard Walker
July 12, 1943–February 15, 1999

More Ready-to-Tell Tales From Around the World

Edited by David Holt and Bill Mooney

August House Publishers, Inc.
LITTLE ROCK

Published 2000 by August House Publishers, Inc.,
P.O. Box 3223, Little Rock, Arkansas, 72203,
501-372-5450

Permissions are included in the Acknowledgments following the text.

Printed in the United States of America

10 9 8 7 6 5 4 3 2 1 HC
10 9 8 7 6 5 4 3 2 1 PB

Library of Congress Cataloging-in-Publication Data
More ready-to-tell tales from around the world /
edited by David Holt and Bill Mooney.
p. cm.
Summary: A multicultural collection of traditional tales contributed by experienced storytellers, with tips for telling the stories
ISBN 0-87483-592-5 (alk. paper) —
ISBN 0-87483-583-6 (trade pbk.)
1. Tales. [1. Folklore. 2. Storytelling—Collections.]
I. Holt, David. II. Mooney, William.
PZ8.1 M796 2000
398.2—dc21 00-032787

Executive Editor: Liz Parkhurst
Production Editor: Joy Freeman
Editorial Assistants: Jody McNeese Keene, Jenny Counts
Cover Design: Harvill Ross Studios, Ltd.
Cover Photo: Cindy Momchilov, Camera Work

On the cover: students from August House's Partner in Education, Gibbs Magnet School of International Studies and Foreign Languages

The paper used in this publication meets the minimum requirements of the American National Standards for Information Sciences—permanence of Paper for Printed Library Materials, ANSI.48-1984.

AUGUST HOUSE PUBLISHERS LITTLE ROCK

Contents

TRICKSTER TALES

TALL TALES

HOW AND WHY TALES

SERVED WITH A TWIST

FAMILY AND COMMUNITY

BENEDICTION

Introduction

DAVID HOLT AND BILL MOONEY

We, as professional storytellers, know how difficult it is to find a really good story—a sure-fire story that you enjoy telling over and over again. It takes a heap of searching and good detective work. It also takes time to understand how the story works and how it should best be told. Sometimes, trying to find a needle in a haystack seems an easier task. That is why we have asked some of the world's finest storytellers to contribute genuinely ready-to-tell tales to serve as a gift to the general storytelling community. This anthology offers you the prospect of no detective work and a haystack over-flowing with needles. The diverse stories are sharp and to the point, honed by countless tellings. Not only that, they "kick in" fast. Every storyteller in the world knows the importance of involving an audience right away. Our anthology offers you a wide variety of stories that will be effective every time you tell them. The first book in this series included only a few international tales, but this collection is literally from around the world.

The only thing we ask in return for using these ready-to-tell tales is that you acknowledge our contributors and tell your audiences something about them and the origins of their story. Use each of the stories as a tribute to the generous gift these storytellers have given you.*

Our contributors have submitted stories from a number of diverse cultures that will appeal to various age levels (they specify for what ages the stories are most appropriate). Through such diverse cultural windows we are better able to understand our universal humanity. While most of the stories are simple to tell, a few will be a bit more challenging. All of them, however, are guaranteed to work. The authors have included telling tips and story background to help you bring the tales to life.

This series of Ready-To-Tell books has been devised to encourage the free

*This permission applies only to oral tellings, not to recordings, printed matter, or any other fixed form of expression. For that, you must contact the author.

trade of good "tellable" tales. Our guideline for this book comes from an old Turkish saying: "Three golden apples fell from the tree. One is for me who told the story, one is for you who listened to the story, and the third I take in my right hand and throw over my left shoulder to all the people who told the story before me." While you can take these specific stories and re-tell them exactly as they are printed here, you will find greater success if you put the stories in your own words and infuse them with your unique personality. Use these stories as good examples, learning from our contributors how they shaped and honed the tales to fit their own individual telling style. Then go thou and do likewise.

In certain cultures, tellers "own" their stories, and other people are not allowed to tell them. In England, there is no traditional ownership of traditional stories. In certain European cultures, however, particularly among the Travelers of Scotland, a teller has to be given his or her stories. In America, our attitude is governed by copyright law and professional courtesy, which dictate that you must not use other people's stories without their permission. There is also an underlying feeling that, if you call yourself a storyteller, you must ferret out your own material. That's part of your job.

Dovie Thomason cautions, "You may use my bones but not my flesh," meaning that the bare-bones plot of a folktale is everyone's property, but not her way of telling it (or, as the copyright law states: her "fixed form of expression."). Laura Simms says, "There are thousands of folktales, told in a variety of ways, that have no ownership because the same story can be found in many cultures. Then there are more sacred stories that certain cultures feel they own. It is not always a black-and-white situation." Laura has come to realize that "ownership has to do with the performance and rendition of a story. The 'bones' of a story has to be brought to life by a particular teller. A memorized tale taken verbatim from a book does not seem like a storytelling piece to me, but it does have ownership because of the way it was written by the author. It's the same for a performance. I find it painful and sad when someone copies my exact language and way of telling, using it as if it were a pre-packaged product. To bring a story to life, you have to infuse it with your own presence, as well as train yourself to read the meaning beneath the words (which manifests itself only through the listening other)."

"Every time I give away a story," says English storyteller Taffy Thomas, "I feel I get far more in return. One good story always deserves another. Whenever I tell a story, I feel that the ghosts of all the previous tellers of the tale are standing behind me ready to help. Some of my storyteller friends, however, think they might be there to strangle me if I don't do justice to the tale. Actually, I feel that storytelling is a lot like the game of Tag. I am "It" until I tell the story. Then the person who hears the story is "It" until they tell it. And so the chain continues." Dan Keding counsels, "If you hear a story without giving one in exchange, then you're reaping the harvest without sowing the seeds." Amen, say we.

If you find usable stories from this book (and we're sure you will), we urge you to reciprocate by giving one of *your* tales back to the storytelling community. As the Scots Travelers say, "Sing a song, tell a story, show your bum, or out you gang (go)."

—David Holt and Bill Mooney

COMIC TALES

The Barking Mouse

A Folktale from Cuba

ANTONIO SACRE

Recommended audience: All ages.

As a Cuban-America, I grew up speaking Spanish and English, but I was often ridiculed for speaking Spanish. My grandmother Mimi made sure that I was proud of both of my cultures. Where she lived, in little Havana in Miami, I heard the Cubans tell many versions of this story, with the ending always the same. Sometimes it featured a Cuban mouse and an American mouse running into an American cat; other times a mouse from Havana and a *guajiro* (rural) mouse encountered a city cat. Regardless of the details, the story states in a funny way an important part of new life in the United States—language is a key to surviving the difficulties of immigration—while also showing the value of being bilingual.

ANTONIO SACRE was born in Boston to a Cuban father and an Irish-American mother. He uses his bicultural background to create funny, touching, universal stories that appeal to all ages. Antonio entertains nationally with a vast repertoire of stories told in Spanish, in English, or a lively interweaving of both. He has acted on stage, film, and television, and told stories from coast to coast. His storytelling cassette, *Looking for Papito,* won a Parents' Choice Gold Award.

JOE HENSON

THE BARKING MOUSE

Una vez había una familia de ratones.
(Once upon a time there was a family of mice.)

There was Mamá Ratón. Who's that? Momma Mouse.

There was Papá Ratón. Who's that? Papa Mouse.

There was Hermana Ratón. Who's that? Sister Mouse.

And there was Hermano Ratón—Brother Mouse.

They all went on a picnic on a beautiful fall day. When they were finished eating, Hermana and Hermano said, *"Mamá, Papá, vamos a jugar!"* ("We're going to play!")

Mamá said, *"Está bien, pero cuídense, por que en la cerca hay un gato."* ("That's fine, but be careful, because near the fence lives El Gato." Who's that? The cat.)

Hermana and Hermano said, "OK"—which is Spanish for "OK"—and they stayed away from the fence for some time. But Hermana and Hermano had never seen a cat in person before—or in cat, or however you say that. They had read about cats, and seen cats on television, and so their curiosity got the better of them. You know what they say, *Curiosity killed the*... Oh, that's a different thing, but you know what I mean.

So where do you think they went? Right up to the fence.

They peeked through the slats in the fence, and sure enough, there was the cat—big green eyes, long whiskers, a tail that flopped in the grass. The brother was amazed. He said, *"Hermana, es un gato?"*

And the sister said, *"Sí, es un gato!"*

The brother said, *"Hola, gato!"*

The sister said, *"Hola, gato!"*

The cat didn't move a whisker.

The brother got silly. He said, *"Hola, gato flaco!"* (Hello, skinny cat!) He stuck out his tongue and gave a big raspberry.

The sister thought that was funny so she joined in. *"Hola, gato flaco—pphhhlllppphhh!"* Oh, they were having a great time making fun of that cat!

The cat's eyes got smaller. Her tail stopped moving. She stretched her claws into the earth and sprung for the fence, pushing her paws through the slats, swinging at and just barely missing the mice. The mice were scared, but when they saw that the cat couldn't reach them they got bold and made fun of her even more.

The cat sat back on her haunches, jumped as high as she could, and fell—*splat*—right into the top of the fence. She fell down on her side of the fence, pawing at her nose. The mice thought that was the funniest thing in the world. The cat tried again—*"Meow!"*— smashed into the fence.

The mice had tears coming out of their eyes now, they were laughing so hard. The cat walked back slowly, stretched up and stretched down, and leapt again, only this time she led with her claws. She dug her claws into the wood of that fence and clawed her way up. She got to the top, looked down, and snickered—*"Hee hee hee!"*—at the mice.

"Adiós, gato!" yelled the mice, turning away and running for their lives. The cat jumped down. She was gaining on them with every single stride when, with a burst of speed, the mice jumped through some little bushes back to their family.

Breathlessly they said, *"Mamá, Papá, vamanos, por que el gato va a comernos!"* ("We better go, that cat is going to eat us!")

Papá looked around, but he didn't see the cat. Papá got tough. He said, *"Gato, yo no tengo miedo del gato."* ("I'm not scared of the cat.") *"Si el gato viene* (if the cat comes), *yo voy a decir que yo soy Papá Ratón, y yo voy a darle Pow Pow Pow!"*

And just then, the cat jumped through the bushes. Papá froze. "Mamá!" he cried, jumping behind her. Hermano and Hermana jumped behind her, too. The only thing that stood between that cat, and her familia, was Mamá.

Mamá didn't know what to do! But with the courage a mother feels when her family is threatened, she stood up as tall as she could on her tiny back paws, looked into the great green eyes of that cat, took a deep breath, and said, *"Roof roof roooof rooow rooow rooff!"*

That cat stopped, looked all around, turned around, jumped over that fence, and was gone.

Mamá couldn't believe it worked. When she got her family home nice and safe, she said, "You see, kids, it pays to speak another language!"

A WORD FROM THE WISE

The Spanish in the story is easy to learn and pronounce and adds a lot to the flavor. Your Spanish-speaking audience members will greatly appreciate the effort you have taken in learning the correct words and pronunciation. You'll be surprised how many people, children included, already know the simple vocabulary of this story; often, by the time Papá is boasting about fighting the cat, the audience won't need a direct translation.

You can perhaps puff out your chest and deepen your voice to show that Papá is not scared of anything, and move your fists in the air for the "Pow Pow Pows" to indicate a tough Papá mouse.

I have a great time when the mice make fun of the cat, though it's important that it not get too mean-spirited. I also try to physicalize the cat in a distinct way by making my hands the claws and putting on a Cheshire grin. You can make the cat's pawing through the fence a bit of a jump at the audience to show how dangerous the situation is for the mice. When the cat gets to the top of the fence, take your time and relish the cat's new situation. When Mamá finally stands up to the cat, make her "bark" as vicious and realistic as possible. You should be as surprised as the cat when Mamá barks. Take your time here—give the audience a moment to realize what has just happened—then tell her final line directly to the audience.

Why Armadillos Are Funny

Adapted from a Folktale from Guyana

BARBARA McBRIDE-SMITH

Recommended audience: Grades K–2. The song seems to appeal to all ages.

This story is my own original and expanded retelling of a folktale from Guyana, South America. I first discovered a minuscule version of it on a tag attached to an armadillo puppet a friend gave me for Christmas. Although I rarely use puppets in my storytelling, I decided to make an exception in this little fella's case. I named him Apollo, and with the help of kids in my school, I developed a repertoire of stories about his silly adventures. This was the first.

BARBARA MCBRIDE-SMITH is a public school librarian and an adjunct seminary professor in Tulsa, Oklahoma. Born in Texas and educated in Massachusetts, she now travels the United States delighting audiences of all ages with her re-imagined folktales and post-modern mythology. She has been a featured performer at the National Storytelling Festival in Jonesborough, Tennessee, and served on the Board of Directors for the National Storytelling Association. Her stories have been recorded on five tape albums and published in her book *Greek Myths, Western Style*.

KEN HELT

WHY ARMADILLOS ARE FUNNY

A long time ago, armadillos weren't the same shy, nocturnal critters we know today. They were so proud of themselves, they thought the sun rose and set on their funny little faces. The armadillos were very friendly, and no creature on earth considered them an enemy. Raccoons liked them. Hawks and eagles liked them. Coyotes and bears and dogs liked them. Cats—well, the truth is, cats didn't care one way or the other—but everybody else enjoyed the armadillos' company.

One very homely little armadillo who lived back then was named Apollo. His mother was ugly, his daddy was ugly, and Apollo was uglier than the two of them put together. But, you see, armadillos are intended to be ugly by nature—the uglier the better. So Apollo was just about perfect...for an armadillo.

Apollo Armadillo discovered when he was just a little tyke that he was particularly talented at being funny. When he bugged out his eyes and waggled his tongue, the other animals fell all over themselves laughing. The squirrels snickered, the iguanas giggled, even the rattlesnakes shook all over with laughter.

One day, Apollo created a new trick to make his friends laugh. He hid in a ditch and waited for an animal to come down the road. The first one who came speeding along was roadrunner. "Beep-beep! Beep-beep!"

When the roadrunner was right next to Apollo's hiding place, the little armadillo dashed out into the road, leapt straight up into the air with his arms and legs spread out in four directions—his hair standing on end, shell jiggling, eyes bugged out, tongue waggling. "*Waaah!*" bellowed Apollo.

The roadrunner came to a screeching halt. "*Arrrgh!*" yelled the roadrunner. Then, *thunk,* he plopped over backwards. He lay there in the road in a cross-eyed daze. After a minute or two, roadrunner picked himself up, saw how silly Apollo looked, and began to laugh. The other animals, watching from the bushes, joined in the fun. Everybody hee-hawed till their sides ached.

Apollo was enormously pleased with himself. His parents were proud, too. They even encouraged his outrageous behavior.

His daddy said, "Son, in my opinion, you could use a little more shtick. Try these. They're a real hoot." (*Storyteller puts on large plastic eyeglasses with attached nose & mustache.)*

Now when he played that same jump-up trick, Apollo looked even funnier than before. He could stop any creature, big or small, and make him laugh.

Down the road came a bouncing bunny.

Boing-boing, Boing-boing.

"*Waaah!*" bellowed Apollo.

"*Arrrgh!*" yelled the bunny. Then, *thunk,* the bunny plopped over backwards.

Down the road came a trotting turkey.

"Trot-trot, gobble-gobble, trot-trot, gobble-gobble."

"*Waaah!*"

"*Arrrgh!*" *Thunk* went the turkey, as he plopped over backwards.

Apollo even stopped a stampeding buffalo.

Down the road came the buffalo.

Galumph, galumph, galumph.

"*Waaah!*"

"*Arrrgh!*" *Thunk,* the buffalo plopped over backwards.

Every time this happened, the dazed animal would pull itself together, get an eyeful of that silly-looking Apollo and start to laugh—softly at first, and then right out loud. No doubt about it, that armadillo had some powerful humor.

But Apollo's mother believed that good can always be better. "Try these on for size," she said. *(Storyteller puts on a funny hat and oversize necktie.)* "Oh my, yes, much improved."

Apollo went down to the roadside again and waited. Along came a big fat possum.

Hunker-cha, hunker-cha, hunker-cha.

Apollo jumped up. "*Waaah!*"

"*Arrrgh!*" And *thunk* went the possum.

Meanwhile up in the sky world, Lightning, who was mean enough to scare night into day, was growing angry. She was supposed to be the only one powerful enough to stop an earth creature in its tracks and make it keel over in shock. That ridiculous-looking armadillo named Apollo was stealing her thunder and she was jealous.

"Thinks he's funny, does he? Well, I'll show that miserable little mammal a thing or two about what's funny!"

The next time Apollo went down to hide beside the road and tickle the wits out of a passerby, Lightning followed him. She darted behind clouds, keeping her presence a secret. Apollo squatted in the ditch, chuckling to himself, waiting for a friendly victim. Suddenly Lightning leapt out from behind a cloud, grabbed a bolt from her quiver, and struck Apollo on top of his ugly little noggin.

"*Arrrgh!*" yelled Apollo.

Apollo's eyes began to spin like tops. He stood on his nose, then he danced on his tail. His plates of armor clacked up and down like a set of false teeth. He rolled up into a tight little ball.* *Thunk* he went, and then *plop,* he fainted.

Lightning couldn't keep a straight face. "Ha! He got a charge out of that!" She grinned all over and went back into the clouds.

Some time later, Apollo woke up, looked around, and couldn't see a thing. "Help! Where am I? Why is it so dark?" Then he realized he was rolled up inside his own armored shell. He stretched and pushed, but he couldn't release himself. He was locked up tight from fright. He shifted his weight back and forth, back and forth, until he began to roll. He rolled down, down, down a hill, hurtling so fast he couldn't stop... until he hit a big oak tree.

Boinnnk!

Crrraaack!

Apollo's shell split in nine places. Did you know that to this day you can still see those cracks on an armadillo's back? Out popped Apollo's nose and feet. And then...

Clunk-clunk-clunkety-clunkety-clunk! Thousands of acorns rained down on his head. Poor little armadillo. At first, he was terribly embarrassed. But Apollo was a trouper. He leapt to his hind legs, smiled at the crowd gathered around him, and took a bow. "Thank you, thank you, my friends. I'm glad you enjoyed my trick!"

All the animals who had seen the commotion began to laugh and applaud. Even Lightning couldn't hold back her laughter. Next thing she knew, she was cackling like a chicken. And then it dawned on her that Apollo was taking all the credit for her joke. She reached into her quiver and fired another fierce bolt at him. But her laughter threw off her aim. The bolt hit the ground, sparks flew, the grass sizzled, and the dirt cracked open. Guess what crawled out of the ground? Earthworms!

*This is a myth. Only the South American three-banded armadillo can curl up into a ball.

"Yum yum, time for dinner!" Apollo grabbed a handful of those wigglies. He slurped up the earthworms, rudely chewing with his mouth open, worms dribbling down his chin, his eyes bugged out in delight.

All the animals convulsed in laughter. "He's disgusting...and so funny!"

And then, *thunk,* they plopped over backwards laughing.

Lightning knew then that Apollo had won their game of wits. She couldn't get the best of him. Lightning went back up into the sky world and never bothered the armadillos on earth again.

And that's how Apollo, a funny little armadillo, taught all the other animals something important: sometimes the best protection from an enemy...is to make the enemy laugh.

You can add this part...or not.

I'm sorry to say this story has a very sad epilogue. Armadillos kept their friends entertained for many years with the trick they learned from Apollo. But then one day, a new creature called an automobile came down the road...

Here's a silly song to honor all the armadillos who have tried and failed to stop a car in its tracks.

THE ARMADILLO SONG
(Tune: "O Tannenbaum")

Chorus:
Oh Armadillo, you're so bold,
Why did you try to cross the road?

1.
You were my friend and now you're dead,
You bear the mark of tire tread.
(Chorus)

2.
You did not see yon passing car,
Now you are spread upon the tar.
(Chorus)

3.
You ran upon the yellow line,
Now you are just a streak of slime.
(Chorus)

4.
I always knew you had few brains,
Now they are spread across two lanes.
(Chorus)

5.
Just like this song, your life is o'er,
That's all there is, there ain't no more!
(Chorus)

A WORD FROM THE WISE

You don't need an armadillo puppet to tell the story. I often tell it without Apollo's assistance. But if your audience has never seen an armadillo, you may want to show them a picture of this odd critter. Be sure to encourage the students to join you in the sound effects. They can even add more animals and create sounds for them.

The song is my own version of a folksong, sometimes sung as "Tom the Toad," which I learned during my son's boy scouting years. The scouts and a decade of students at my school in Oklahoma have written dozens of delightfully disgusting verses for the armadillo version. If armadillos are not found in your locale, try writing a similar song about skunks, possums, or other roadkill.

The Three Wishes

A Folktale from Sweden

MARTHA HAMILTON AND MITCH WEISS

Recommended audience: Grades K–5.

We found versions of this story ranging from Puerto Rico to France to Korea. In his *More English Fairy Tales,* Joseph Jacobs says he believes all of the variants originally derived from India.

Being a husband and wife duo, we have always been attracted to stories about couples. Fortunately, there are many found throughout world folklore. This story works especially well when told by a man and a woman. However, in our work in the classroom we've also seen it told successfully by children, whether singly or in pairs.

Martha Hamilton and Mitch Weiss are a husband-and-wife storytelling team who live in Ithaca, New York. They have been performing together as Beauty & the Beast Storytellers throughout the United States, Canada, and Europe since 1980. (It's up to their audiences to decide which one is the Beauty and which the Beast.) In addition to their performances, they are known for their school residencies, where they teach students to tell stories. They have written *Children Tell Stories: A Teaching Guide,* which received an Anne Izard Storytellers' Choice Award; and *Stories in My Pocket: Tales Kids Can Tell,* which received a 1997 Storytelling World Award. Their cassette of the same name

DEDE HATCH

received a 1998 Parents' Choice Recommendation as well as a Gold Award from The National Association of Parenting Publication Awards. They also authored *How and Why Stories: World Tales Kids Can Read and Tell,* a 1999 Storytelling World Winner, and recently produced a companion recording by the same name.

THE THREE WISHES

A poor woodsman lived with his wife in a tiny hut. Though he chopped wood every day, he never seemed to sell enough to buy any of the things they needed. Often he and his wife went hungry. One day as the woodcutter raised his ax to a huge oak tree, he heard a voice call out, "Stop! Please don't cut my tree down!"

The woodcutter looked up and saw a tree spirit high in the branches. Though he had heard of tree spirits, he had never actually seen one. He dropped his ax to the ground and listened as the spirit pleaded, "Please, sir, I have guarded this tree for over a hundred years, and I beg you not to cut it down."

The woodcutter hesitated. He knew the tree would be worth a good sum of money. At last he replied, "Oh, all right. If it's yours, I guess I have no right to chop it down."

With great relief, the tree spirit said, "Thank you! And since you've been so kind, I'll grant you and your wife three wishes. No matter what you wish for, your next three wishes will come true."

The woodcutter opened his mouth, but before he could say a word, the tree spirit had vanished. He hurried home to his wife. "Dear, you won't believe what happened. A tree spirit appeared and promised that it would grant us three wishes! Just imagine—any three wishes we want! We're in luck!"

"Have you lost your mind?" replied his wife. "Tree spirits? Wishes? Go back to work and stop your dreaming!"

"But, wife, it's true! Let's put it to the test and see what happens. Just think...we could wish for a pot of gold!"

"Why sure," said his wife in a scornful tone. "I suppose we could wish for a mansion with servants. We could wish for a lot of things."

"Like a chest full of diamonds and rubies and pearls, or clothes made of the finest silks and satins," said the husband excitedly.

"Or for something good to eat," grumbled the wife. "Anything besides potatoes, which is all we ever seem to eat."

"Now that's a wish that would please my empty stomach!" cried the husband. "I am so hungry! I wish I had a nice big juicy sausage right now!"

Lo and Behold! At that very instant a huge sausage appeared right on the table. It was at least five feet long. The woodcutter and his wife were very surprised to see it.

"So it is true!" his wife squealed with delight. "We do have three wishes!" But in the next moment her tone changed to anger. "Oh, you fool! You've wasted one of our wishes on a sausage. You could've had a whole pig! You could've had a whole farm, with hundreds of pigs!"

"I guess I didn't think."

"You nincompoop! You never think. You wished for a sausage and wasted a wish! Now we only have two wishes left."

"I'm sorry," said the husband. "But we can still ask for a mansion and a pot of gold."

"But we can't ask for a chest of jewels or fancy clothes—or anything else for that matter! What a foolish thing to do! Who else would rather have a sausage than a chest of jewels? Oh, I am so mad! I wish that sausage was hanging from the end of your nose!"

Lo and Behold! The sausage suddenly hung from the end of her husband's nose, all the way down to his toes. The woman took one look at him and burst out laughing.

But the woodcutter was not amused. "Oh, how foolish you are! And how ridiculous I must look! First I make a little mistake, and now you make it twice as bad. Now our second wish is gone."

"It's true I wished without thinking. But we could still wish for a pot of gold. We do have one wish left."

"Yes, but what good are riches if I have a sausage hanging from the end of my nose for the rest of my life? I look like an elephant with a long trunk. And it's all your fault! Now help me get it off."

They pulled and tugged at that sausage. They even tried to cut it, but no matter what they did, the sausage would not budge. At last the woman knew what their third wish had to be. "Oh, I wish that sausage wasn't hanging from your nose!"

Lo and Behold! Instantly the sausage fell from the man's nose onto the table. And that was the last of their three wishes. They never had a pot of gold, or a mansion, or a chest of jewels. But at least they were able to enjoy a good sausage supper.

If someone should happen to give *you* three wishes, remember this story. Don't waste them like the woodcutter and his wife.

A WORD FROM THE WISE

A good deal of this story consists of dialogue between a husband and a wife. Whether you are telling the story with a partner or by yourself, you will want to omit the repetition of "he said, she said," which is awkward in an oral telling. If you aren't working with a partner, you will need to show with body language that two different people are speaking. Hold your body differently for each character, or make the two voices distinct. You may want to also turn your head and upper body slightly to one side when speaking as the wife, then to the other for the husband. Don't turn too far or your voice will project to the side rather than out toward the audience.

If you are telling the story with a partner, one of you should be the woodcutter, and the other both the tree spirit and the wife. When we tell the story together, we like to say "Lo and Behold!" in tandem.

The Young and Dashing Princess

A Fractured Fairy Tale

BETH HORNER

Recommended audience: Grades K–5 and adults. Great for families and mixed-age audiences.

This participation story is a take-off on "The King With the Terrible Temper," a one-paged story that can be found in camp manuals. When I was a librarian, I read it in *With A Deep Sea Smile* by Virginia Tashjian, a wonderful book full of participation stories. I publish this updated version with Ms. Tashjian's permission. In "The King With the Terrible Temper," a prince seeking a bride comes to the king's castle, where he finds three princesses—one being too fat, one too thin, and one just right. The prince selects the "just right" princess and takes her away against the king's wishes. I have turned the story around, changed the defining characteristics of the three choices, and added humor as well as a slightly modern slant to the story. It works very well with elementary, adult, and mixed-age audiences. It is not a deep, enduring story. Rather, it provides a good break in a program and is a lot of fun.

RON GURULÉ

BETH HORNER is a former children's librarian and nationally acclaimed storyteller, writer, lecturer, and recording artist. With her high-energy performances, punctuated with music and humor, she has performed at the National Storytelling Festival and at meetings of the American Library Association and the National Council of Teachers of English. Beth's goals as a storyteller are to entertain, educate, and empower—which she accomplishes with a repertoire of traditional and contemporary tales, and original stories drawn from her own ancestry. Through her workshops and seminars on Integrating Music into Storytelling and Storytelling to Teens, Beth has inspired many to stretch beyond their traditional concept of storytelling. Beth's recordings include *An Evening At Cedar Creek, Mothers & Other Wild Women,* and the ever-popular *Encounter With A Romance Novel.*

THE YOUNG AND DASHING PRINCESS

There was once a *king with a terrible temper.*
(GRRRRR)

He had three sons. One of the sons was not what one would call highly motivated. He would arise at approximately twelve noon each day, descend the stairs one... by one... by one, and partake of a cup of tea. If he was feeling full of vim and vigor, he would perhaps then take a brief stroll in the garden before ascending the stairs one... by one... by one and returning to bed. He was not quite "upwardly mobile." This was the *first son.*

(KA-PLUNK... KA-PLUNK... KA-PLUNK... KA-PLUNK)

Then there was another son. He *was* highly motivated. He *was* upwardly mobile. He *was* extremely energetic. Each day he would *leap* out of bed, bound down the stairs two... three... four steps at a time and be busy, busy, busy all day! And, as he was doing things, he would speak constantly about what it was that he was doing. He would tell you all about the great things that he had done, all about the great and wonderful things that he was currently doing, and all about the great, wonderful and incredible things that he was going to do in the near future. In addition, he wore all the right clothes, cruised all the right malls, and worked out once... twice... *three* times a day. He was so energetic, so highly motivated, so upwardly mobile that he was going to be a doctor, a lawyer, an engineer, *and* a vegetarian chef. He was the *second son!*

(AAAAACK)

Of course, there was one more son. We will discover him later in the story. He was the *third son.*

(WHEW... AAAH)

One day, the mighty monarch was mounted upon his marvelous throne when he heard something approaching the castle. It was a *galloping horse.*

(HAND SLAPS)

There was a bold *knock upon the door.*

(KNOCKING SOUND)

Opening the door, the king found standing there a *young and dashing princess.*

(TA-DUM!)

"What do you want?" said the *king with the terrible temper.*

(GRRRRR)

"Hello, King," said the *young and dashing princess,*

(TA-DUM!)

"I live in the next land. My parents, the King and the Queen, are getting ready to retire. So, I am about to take the throne. I have watched my parents rule the land together for lo these many years and they've done well together. I was thinking that it might be nice to have someone to rule by my side. So, I'm looking around, if you know what I mean, and I hear that you have some sons here."

"Indeed I do," said the *king with the terrible temper.*

(GRRRRR)

"In fact, I have just the one for you!" Going to the bottom of the stairs, he called down the *first son,*

(KA-PLUNK... KA-PLUNK... KA-PLUNK... KA-PLUNK)

who descended the stairs one... by one... by one.

"I have three questions for you," said the *young and dashing princess.*

(TA-DUM!)

"The first question: if there were poor and needy in the land, how would you feed and shelter them?"

"Hmmmm," mused the prince. "Well, I'd have a cup of tea and contemplate the matter."

"I see," said the princess thoughtfully. "Second question: what do you think would be the best way for us to budget our gold to ensure that we would have enough for our old age?"

"Hmmm," mused the prince. "Well, first I'd have a cup of tea and then, contemplate the matter."

"I see," said the princess thoughtfully. "Third question: if we had children, would you be willing to attend each and every one of their soccer games?"

"Oh," said the prince. "Well, I'd have to have a cup of tea and contemplate the matter."

"King," announced the *young and dashing princess,*

(TA-DUM!)

"I am not marrying your *first son.*"

(KA-PLUNK... KA-PLUNK... KA-PLUNK... KA-PLUNK)

"Rats!" said the *king with the terrible temper.*

(GRRRRR)

"Never fear!" he said. "I have another son!" Going to the bottom of the stairs, he called down the *second son,*

(AAAAACK)

who bounded down the stairs two... three... four steps at a time, leapt to the bottom, and announced, "Princess, I am the one for you!"

"Ah," said the *young and dashing princess.*

(TA-DUM!)

"But first a few questions. If there were poor and needy in the land, how would you feed and shelter them?"

"Well, that's easy," exclaimed the prince. "I'd tell them to get off their duffs and get to work! They need to get out there and get a job. If they'd just fix themselves up and look better they'd have a better chance of doing so. They should be like me! I wear all the right clothes and cruise all the right malls. I work out once... twice... THREE times a day. That's what they should do!"

"I see," said the princess thoughtfully. "Second question: what do you think would be the best way to budget our gold to ensure that we would have enough for our old age?"

"Honey," said the prince, "with me at your side, you wouldn't have to worry your pretty little princess head about managing the gold. I'd handle all of that. Don't you even give it a second thought."

"I see," said the princess. "Third and final question: if we were to have children, would you be willing to attend each and every one of their soccer games?"

"Well, I won't have the time, my dear," said the prince. "I am going to be busy, busy, busy! I'm going to do great and wonderful things with my life, you know. After all, I'm going to be a doctor, a lawyer, an engineer and a vegetarian chef!"

"King," said the *young and dashing princess,*

(TA-DUM!)

"I will not be marrying your *second son!*"

(AAAAACK)

"Rats!" said the *king with the terrible temper.*

(GRRRRR)

"Well, I'm sorry, princess," said the king. "That's all the sons in this castle."

"But I was told that you had three sons," said the princess.

"No! No! I don't!" said the king. But at that moment, the princess looked up. There, descending the stairs was a young man with a book in one hand—and in the other hand, a basket of laundry.

"Who's that?" asked the princess.

"No one. No one," exclaimed the *king with the terrible temper.*

(GRRRRR)

"It is time for you to leave!"

But the princess ascended the stairs, engaged the young man in conversation, and learned that, in truth, it was the *third son.*

(WHEW...AAAH)

The two began to talk. They discussed the book that he was reading. They discussed the laundry that he was carrying. They spoke of the poor and needy, of the problems involved in budgeting gold, and of children and their soccer games. Then, he told her a joke and she laughed. She told him a joke and he laughed. In short, they fell in love.

"King," announced the *young and dashing princess,*

(TA-DUM!)

"I am going to marry your *third son!"*

(WHEW...AAAH)

"No! No!" exclaimed the *king with the terrible temper.*

(GRRRRR)

"You can't take him away and leave me here with these other two sons! I'll go insane! How do you think I got this terrible temper? Never! Never! Guards! Guards!" he called.

The guards surrounded the hall. However, the *young and dashing princess*

(TA-DUM!)

grabbed the hand of the *third son*

(WHEW...AAAH)

and together they ran down the stairs and out the door. They jumped upon their steeds and galloped away upon their *galloping horses.*

(HAND SLAPS)

"Stop them! Stop them!" cried the *king with the terrible temper.*

(GRRRRR)

"After them! After them!"

The guards ran out the door, jumped upon their steeds and galloped away on their *galloping horses.*

(HAND SLAPS)

The princess and prince galloped upon their *galloping horses.*

(HAND SLAPS)

The guards galloped upon their *galloping horses.*

(HAND SLAPS)

But the prince and princess, sped on by the horses, by love, and by the promise of the future, were soon out of sight and into the next land. It was there that they were married and ruled wisely together. Together, they cared for the poor and needy, enjoyed life while still saving gold for their old age, attended more soccer games than one could count, and lived happily the rest of their days.

And so ends the tale of the *king with the terrible temper,*

(GRRRRR)

his *first son,*
(KA-PLUNK... KA-PLUNK... KA-PLUNK... KA-PLUNK)
his *second son,*
(AAAAACK)
his *third son,*
(WHEW... AAAH)
a *knock upon the door,*
(KNOCKING SOUND)
some *galloping horses,*
(HAND SLAPS)
and a *young and dashing princess.*
(TA-DUM!)

A WORD FROM THE WISE

Before beginning the story, teach the listeners the following sounds and actions that are to be done each time the storyteller speaks the corresponding phrase.

King with a Terrible Temper: GRRRRR
Hands raised like claws

First Son: KA-PLUNK... KA-PLUNK... KA-PLUNK... KA-PLUNK

Second Son: AAAAACK (as if frightened)
Hands waving frantically and fearfully

Third Son: WHEW... AAAH (sigh)
"WHEW" *is accompanied by gesture of relief (back of hand across forehead)*
"AAAH" *is a sigh and accompanied by holding both hands over the heart.*

Knock upon the Door: any sort of KNOCKING SOUND

Galloping Horses: HAND SLAPS on lap

Young and Dashing Princess: TA-DUM!
Accompanied by raising one's arms in old-fashioned "muscle man" style

Pacing is important. When speaking of or as the first son, I recommend a slow, methodical pace. When speaking of or as the second son, I recommend a fast, frenetic pace. I also recommend representing the king as angry and the princess as bold.

The three questions that the princess asks the first two sons can be changed to anything that would be fun and appropriate for your particular audience. When telling to an adult audience, I often create questions that humorously reflect the current political scene. If I am telling to a primary-aged children's audience, I might ask a question such as "Would you be willing to eat spinach with every meal?" or "Would you be willing to sleep with worms under your pillow?" Keep in mind that although the first son's answers always remain the same no matter the question, the second son's answers must correspond to the selected questions.

Feel free to speak the phrases that require audience participation as rarely or frequently as you feel is best. The frequency will depend upon the age and size of your audience. I recommend that you experiment and have fun with it.

The Belly Button Monster

A Traveling Tale from the United States

OLGA LOYA

Recommended audience: Grades K–3 and family audiences.

I heard a version of this story about fifteen years ago from a man I only knew as Arnie. He said he had heard the story from a woman who had heard it from another man. It is the classic situation of a story being passed on. I have never heard the story since then and have been telling my version of it ever since.

OLGA LOYA has performed and taught storytelling workshops all over the United States and Mexico. She has been a featured teller at the First Latin American Storytelling Festival and the National Storytelling Festival in Jonesborough. Loya performs in theaters, universities, festivals, conferences, museums, libraries, and schools. She has created eight videos, two tapes, and a book called *Momentos Mágicos/Magic Moments,* which won an Aesop Accolade, the International Reading Association Young Adults Choice Award, and Honorable Mention by Americas (by the Consortium of Latin American Studies Programs).

DANIEL HERRON STUDIOS

THE BELLY BUTTON MONSTER

Once there was a little boy named Jimmy. Jimmy was a good little boy. He minded his mother, his father, his teachers—everyone. But there was one thing he could not seem to do. He could not seem to keep his blankets on at night. Every night as soon as he relaxed—*swoosh,* he threw his blankets off.

One night his mother came into his room and said, "Jimmy, you have to keep your blankets on you. It has been very cold! You have been sick and you need to keep warm."

"Mama, I will try!" said Jimmy.

He thought, *Maybe I will try to do something different.* So he closed his eyes, his mouth—he tightened everything on his body as much as he could. He held on to his blankets very tightly. But the moment he relaxed, well, you know what happened—*swoosh,* he threw his blankets off.

Jimmy's mama came into his room. She was very upset and said, "Now Jimmy, you will be very sick if you don't keep your blankets on you! Please keep them on!"

"Oh, mama, I am truly trying."

She left his room. He lay there and thought, "Hmmm, last time I tried to keep everything tight, but this time I will open everything up."

So he lay there with his mouth, eyes, arms, legs, and fingers wide open.

But the moment he relaxed, well, you know what happened—*swoosh,* he threw his blankets off.

His mama came into the room, "Now Jimmy, it's very cold and you have been sick. If you don't keep your blankets on, the Belly Button Monster will come and take your belly button away!"

"No, mama. There is no Belly Button Monster!"

As Jimmy's mama walked out she said, "Yes, there is a Belly Button Monster."

Jimmy held onto his blankets with everything wide open. But he could not stay awake. The moment he relaxed, well, you know what happened—*swoosh,* he threw his blankets off.

All this time the Belly Button Monster was flying around looking for the perfect belly button. He landed right by Jimmy and looked at Jimmy's belly button and said, "Oh, that's the nicest looking belly button I have ever seen."

He reached down and plucked Jimmy's belly button. He put it in his belly button bag. You could tell which belly button was Jimmy's because it was the nicest-looking one of all.

The Belly Button Monster happily flew away.

Jimmy woke up the next morning and he didn't know that anything had happened. He went down to the kitchen and filled a glass with milk. He took a nice long drink. What do you suppose happened? Milk poured out of his belly button and into his pajamas and slippers.

He looked down and said, "Yuk."

He decided he would go take a bath. He filled the tub with water. When he got in the tub, his stomach filled up with water. He had to push his hands up against his stomach to get the water out.

Jimmy was very unhappy. He knew he couldn't drink anything, or take a bath. He wondered what else he could not do! Besides, he wanted his belly button back.

He thought, *Maybe if I pretend I am asleep the Belly Button Monster will come back.*

So he closed his eyes. He pretended to relax, and well, you know what happened—*swoosh,* he threw his blankets off.

All this time the Belly Button Monster had been flying around. Suddenly he stopped, and said, "Hmm, I wonder if that little boy has another beautiful belly button."

He flew to Jimmy's house and went and stood over Jimmy, looking for another belly button. Suddenly Jimmy sat up. "Give me back my belly button!" he yelled.

This frightened the Belly Button Monster. No one had ever spoken to him, let alone yelled at him. "Can't you be a little more polite, little boy?" he asked.

Jimmy said, "Oh, please, oh please, won't you give me my belly button back?"

"Oh, all right," said the Belly Button Monster.

He took out his belly button bag. You could tell which one was Jimmy's because it was the nicest-looking one of all.

He held the belly button away from Jimmy and then began to hum as he slowly moved the belly button closer and closer to Jimmy. Suddenly the belly button flew out of the monster's hand and landed on Jimmy's ear.

"Oh no, not on my ear!" yelled Jimmy.

"Why not? It looks rather nice there," said the Belly Button Monster.

"Please, oh please, won't you please put it back in my stomach where it belongs?"

"Oh, all right, I will try."

The Belly Button Monster took the belly button off Jimmy's ear. He held it away from Jimmy. As he began to hum, he slowly moved the belly button closer and closer to Jimmy. Suddenly—the belly button went flying and landed right on Jimmy's nose.

"But I don't want it on my nose," moaned Jimmy.

"Why not?" asked the Belly Button Monster. "Just think. You will be famous. You will be the only little boy with a belly button on your nose."

"I don't want to be famous! I just want my belly button back in my tummy!"

"Oh, all right, I will try. You are such a troublesome little boy."

He took the belly button off of Jimmy's nose. He started to hum as he moved the belly button closer and closer to Jimmy. Suddenly he stopped humming and moving it. Then he started to hum and move the belly button again. He stopped and started until he was very close to Jimmy's tummy. Then the belly button went flying right into Jimmy's tummy.

Jimmy hugged his tummy and said, "Ohhh, that feels so good!"

The Belly Button Monster said, "I'm leaving here and never returning because you are a very troublesome little boy."

The Belly Button Monster flew away.

After that Jimmy never threw his blankets off, because he never ever wanted to see that Belly Button Monster again!

A WORD FROM THE WISE

This story works for kindergarten to third grade. It also works very well in family shows. I usually introduce this story by saying I am going to tell a very serious story. I tell the audience that I want them to get their most serious faces on. I wait until they are all squinching up their faces and then I announce the name of the story: "The Belly Button Monster." They always laugh very hard. As I tell the story I make the *swoosh* sound with an arm movement, as though I am throwing the blankets off. The next time that same line comes up—"The moment he relaxed, well, you know what happened"—I take a pause and then I make the swoosh sound and move my arm. Everytime I repeat the line, more and more children join in, until most of them are making the *swoosh*ing sound and moving their arms.

In the end of the story, when the Belly Button Monster is moving toward Jimmy with the belly button, I use a kind of high hum. I take a pause before I say where it landed. As the Belly Button Monster is moving the belly button toward Jimmy for the third time, I stop to build up tension and also to gently stop the audience remarks—by this time, they are calling out different parts of the body!

This story is a lot of fun to tell, and the audience always seems to enjoy it.

WISE FOOLS

Jean Sot and the Bull's Milk

A Cajun Folktale

J.J. RENEAUX

Recommended audience: Middle school grades.

There are many tales about Jean Sot, or Foolish John. Unlike Jack, the hero of the Appalachian mountain tales, Jean Sot isn't clever at all, but is as slow-witted and gullible as they come. He is always getting into trouble in the silliest ways. His poor *maman* doesn't know what to do with him. But Jean Sot isn't always a loser; sometimes he wins by pure luck. Mr. Lawrence Molleré liked to tell this story in between spitting out long streams of tobacco juice into a Coca-Cola bottle. He'd get a sly grin on his face and hold out the slimy bottle and say, "Wanna Coke?" I never took him up on his offer—after all, I wasn't as silly-headed as Jean Sot!

Nationally acclaimed storyteller J.J. RENEAUX grew up Cajun for true, surrounded by the stories, music, food, superstitions, and culture of rural communities in southeastern Texas and southern Louisiana. Until her recent death, she performed at festivals and universities around the world, including the National Storytelling Festival. Her books include *Cajun Folktales,* which won the Anne Izard Storyteller's Choice Award, *Haunted Bayou and Other Cajun Ghost Stories,* and the picture book *Why Alligator Hates Dog.* Her audiocassettes include *Wake, Snake!,* winner of several prestigious awards such as the Parents' Choice Gold Award, *Cajun Fairy Tales,* and *Cajun Ghost Stories.*

NANCY BENNET EVELYN

JEAN SOT AND THE BULL'S MILK

Down around Mamou, there was once a boy who was so foolish that everybody called him Jean Sot, Foolish John. He and his *maman* were dirt poor, and he was less than no help at all. It seemed like Jean Sot just couldn't do anything right. Everything he touched ended in ruin, and he believed any silly story he was told. His *maman* would shake her head and sigh, "Oh, that boy must have moss between his ears!"

The people in his village loved to tease and play jokes on him. They'd say, "Jean Sot, the sky is fallin'!" The poor thing would run and hide, sure the world was ending for true. But their best joke was to ask, "Hey, boy, whatcha gonna be when you all grown up?"

Jean Sot loved that question. He would grin from ear to ear and say, "Me, I'm gonna marry the prettiest girl and be the richest man in all the parish." How the people laughed and laughed!

In time, the foolish boy became a foolish young man. One day as he was walking down the road, he passed by a big, fancy house. A beautiful girl was sitting up on the *galerie,* combing out her golden hair. She had the face of an angel but the brains of a duck. She was every inch as foolish as Jean Sot! Wouldn't you know, those two took one look at each other and fell right in love.

Jean Sot begged her to marry him. The girl says, "Oh, yes, *cher, mais oui!* But you must ask Papa for my hand!" The foolish boy ran to the girl's daddy, little knowing that this was the richest man in the parish, and asked to marry his daughter. But the rich man knew all too well about Jean Sot, and he had not the least intention of seeing his only child marry a fool, much less a poor one. Still, he thought it might be a good joke to play along and see just how foolish Jean Sot could be.

"Hmm," says the rich man, pretending to think it over, "I don't know if you are good enough for my daughter. Maybe you can prove yourself to me?"

"Oh, *oui,* Papa, anything you say!"

"Well, then, take this silver flask and fill it up for me."

"What do you want?" asks Jean Sot. "Wine, whiskey?"

"Non," says the rich man, keeping a straight face. "Take this flask and fill it up with... bull's milk. That's right! If you can fill this flask with the milk of a bull, then you can marry my daughter, and all my wealth will be yours someday."

So Jean Sot eagerly took the flask, and away he went down the road to find a bull to milk. He ran until he came to the countryside. There in a pasture, sure enough, was a big ol' mean-lookin' bull.

He walked right up to that bull and looked him over, trying to figure where to get started. But ol' bull was getting madder and madder, pawing the ground, shaking his horns. The next thing you know, he was charging and Jean Sot was running for his life. He just barely escaped!

That evening Jean Sot thought harder than he'd ever thought in his life. Suddenly, it came to him. The girl's father had tricked him! Now, after a lifetime of being the target of everyone's practical jokes, even Jean Sot had learned a little something, you see. He thinks, "The time has come to show them all." Soon he had made a plan.

Late that night, with a little hatchet in hand, he went back to the rich man's house and shimmied up a slippery willow tree growing beside the man's bedroom window. He perched on a limb and took to chopping on that tree, chip-chop, chip-chop, chip-chop. All the while he's moanin' and groanin', "Oh, *mon pauvre papa!* Oh, my poor *papa!*"

Before long, the whole neighborhood came running to see what all the commotion was about.

The shutters of the rich man's window flew open and he hollered out, "Jean Sot, is that you? What the devil are you doin', choppin' on my tree and moanin' to raise the dead in the middle of the night? I know you're foolish, but I didn't know you was crazy too!"

"Oh, my poor *papa,* he's havin' such a hard time of it," said Jean Sot. "This bark'll make a good tea, don't ya know, and help 'im get stronger."

"What's the matter with your *papa,* boy?" asked the rich man, taken aback. "Is he sick-sick? Has he got the fever?"

"Oh, no, it's much worse than that!" said Jean Sot. "Never has a poor man had it so rough. You see, tonight my *papa* gave birth—to twins!"

"Mon Dieu!" the rich man exclaimed. "Did he have boys, girls, or one of each?"

With that, Jean Sot started in to laughin' so hard he nearly fell out of the tree. The neighbors were slappin' each other on the back and sputterin'. Well, the rich man realized he'd been had, and he starts to cussin'.

"Of all the... Jean Sot, you better get outta that tree and quit tellin' lies 'fore I get my shotgun after you!"

"I don't think I'd be talkin' 'bout lyin' if I was you," said Jean Sot. "I don't want to call you a liar, but if you say a bull can give milk, then my *papa* can give birth to twins, for true!"

The rich man was ashamed. His neighbors had witnessed the whole thing, and so he was forced to hold up his end of the bargain or be ridiculed as a greater fool than Jean Sot.

And so, just as he had predicted, Jean married the prettiest girl and became the richest man in the whole parish. The people started thinking that he must really be smart-smart after all. They even made him captain of the Mardi Gras riders. It just goes to show that even the greatest of fools can sometimes become a leader.

A WORD FROM THE WISE

Kids love the idea of a fool wising up and turning the tables on his bully. In the scene where Jean Sot tries to milk the bull there is a lot of room for humorous interpretation. I focus on the bull's reaction, adding many facial expressions, sound effects, and gestures to indicate the bull's surprise, anger, and rage. Let the listener fill in the pictures of what Jean Sot is trying to accomplish with the bull. Adding cultural information about the prairie Mardi Gras will help listeners put the story in context.

A Chelm Medley

Comic Tales from the Jewish Tradition

SYD LIEBERMAN

Recommended audience: Family shows.

In the Jewish tradition there is a town called Chelm, a town of fools. I'm drawn to tales about Chelm for three reasons. First, I like a story that has a laugh in it, and there is a lot to laugh about when you deal with the Chelmites. Second—and I hate to say this—I can identify with their foolishness. I don't think I've ever been as silly as the Chelmites, but I've come close. And finally, in some odd way, the Chelmites' thinking is actually very logical even if completely foolish. That's part of the fun of these stories. To show you what I mean, let me tell you about Mendel, the *shammas* (the synagogue caretaker) in Chelm.

SYD LIEBERMAN is an internationally acclaimed storyteller, author, and award-winning teacher. His seven audiocassettes have garnered five awards from the American Library Association and two from Parents' Choice. He has authored two books: *Streets and Alleys: Stories with a Chicago Accent,* a book of his personal stories; and *The Wise Shoemaker of Studena,* a picture book. He has taught English for thirty years. In 1986, the Golden Apple Foundation for Excellence in Teaching awarded him a Golden Apple for his work in the classroom. He and his wife, Adrienne, live in Evanston, Illinois.

SHERWOOD FOHRMAN

Syd Lieberman

A CHELM MEDLEY

Mendel was the kind of man who, when he went to the sweat bath on Friday night, was afraid to take his clothes off. You see, he thought if he took his clothes off, he'd forget who he was. So what did he do? He tied a string around his legs so he'd remember. But when he got into the sweat bath, the string fell off. Mendel looked up and there sat another man with a string tied around his leg. He, too, was afraid he'd forget who he was. When Mendel looked at the second man, he said, "Oh, my God, if you're me, who am I?"

Another time, Mendel was walking down the road when a stranger came up to him and said, "Take this, Yankel." Then he punched Mendel. Mendel fell to the ground. As soon as he hit the ground, he began laughing. The stranger said, "What are you laughing about? I just punched you. I knocked you on the ground."

Mendel looked up and said, "The joke's on you. I'm not Yankel!"

Once Mendel was looking out the window of his house, watching his wife wash his underwear. Well, in those days, you dipped your clothes in the river and then you put them on a rock and you beat them and beat them and beat them. His wife took his underwear and put it in the river and then on the rock and beat it and beat it and beat it. Then back it went in the river and back on the rock, where she beat it and beat it and beat it again. Finally, after about the fifth time, Mendel looked up and said, "Blessed be Thou, O Lord, who gave me the wisdom to get out of my underwear—just in time."

Once, Mendel was heading into Warsaw with his arms outstretched and his thumbs pointing up rigidly about nine inches apart. When people saw him walking down the road, they said, "Look at the poor cripple, paralyzed, with his arms straight out. My, what a hard life he must have."

Now, when he arrived at the wagon, he said to the wagon driver, "Please, could you reach into my pockets and get the money out? You know, for obvious reasons." The wagon driver thought, *What a pity, a poor man, paralyzed like this with his thumbs out.* So the wagon driver got down, reached into his pocket, and took his money. He even lifted Mendel up onto the wagon. All of the people treated him with respect and dignity. They all thought about his hard life. So when they stopped, they helped him down, and when they started again, they put him back up. When they ate, he opened his mouth and they put food in. All the way to Warsaw it was like this. Finally one woman asked him, just as they were pulling in, "Uncle, how long have you been inflicted with this paralysis?"

"What?" Mendel replied. "What paralysis? I'm not paralyzed. My wife knew I was going to Warsaw. She wanted me to buy her a pair of shoes. This is the size of her foot. You don't know my wife. If I got the wrong size, she would make my life miserable."

Another time, Mendel was heading into Warsaw. This time he used his own wagon and horse because he didn't have to keep his thumbs in the air. On the way he stopped at an inn. A man at the inn realized Mendel was a Chelmite and knew he could trick him and cheat him. The man quickly disappeared with Mendel's horse, rode to a nearby town, and sold the horse to a horse trader.

After the meal, Mendel came out and found the man who sold his horse standing in the horse's harness. Mendel looked at him and said, "What are you doing? What happened to my horse?"

The man said, "My name is Motl, and I am your horse. I've been your horse for ten years. I used to be a man, but I was so sinful, God turned me into a horse. But for the last ten years, I've been praying and I've been repenting, and today, he turned me back into a human."

Mendel said, "Oh, my God, how wonderful! Wonderful! God bless you! Go have a good life. Only Motl, you know you shouldn't sin anymore."

Now as soon as the man left, Mendel realized he had a problem: no horse. So what did he do? He went into the horse trader's. And what did he find? His horse.

As soon as he saw his horse, Mendel slapped himself, his eyes opened wide, and he said, "Oy, Motl, not ten minutes and already you're sinning?"

A WORD FROM THE WISE

These five short pieces tend to read like jokes. You can expand a story, but the result never seems worth the punchline. I put these together to create the feeling of Chelm. In my mind, they work as one story. I tell them all in concert.

Let your audience know that funny material is coming by telling them that these are stories about foolish people. Knowing that will get them ready to laugh. Though these tales work as jokes, the punchlines work only if they are delivered seriously.

The funny part of a Chelm tale is that the Chelmite really believes what he is saying. And if you think about the stories, they do contain a kind of absurd logic. Think of the way Jack Benny would deliver his punch lines. You're after that deadpan approach. Chelm stories are great for family shows because both children and adults love them. By the way, pronounce the *ch* in Chelm as if you were clearing your throat.

Juan Bobo's Pig

A Folktale from Puerto Rico

JOSEPH SOBOL

Reccommended audience: Grades K–5.

I adapted this story from a version told to me by a Spanish bilingual teacher during a high school residency in Chicago. The story was one of her favorites from her Puerto Rican childhood. Juan Bobo tales are as well known in Puerto Rico as Jack tales in Appalachia, and Juan Bobo is a lot like the Foolish Jack of tales like "Jack's First Job." The harder he tries to follow adults' instructions in tale after tale, the bigger the mess he makes of them.

JOSEPH DANIEL SOBOL has worked for nearly two decades as a professional storyteller, musician, and folklorist. He has published an epic study of the American storytelling movement called *The Storytellers' Journey: An American Revival.* He has told and collected traditional tales and tunes in the Carolinas, Ireland, and the immigrant communities of Chicago. Joseph has also toured the United States with his original musical theater piece, *In the Deep Heart's Core,* based on the works of Irish poet W.B. Yeats.

BILL BURLINGHAM

JUAN BOBO'S PIG

Have you heard the story of Juan Bobo and his pig?

Once upon a time in a little village in Puerto Rico, there was a little boy named Juan Bobo. One day Juan Bobo's mother said to him, "*Juanito mijo,* go and clean up the pig and make her look as beautiful as you can, so that when you take her to market this morning to sell her she will fetch a good price."

Well, Juan Bobo always tried to do exactly as his mother told him. So he went and washed the pig with buckets of soapy water, and scrubbed her face with a warm washcloth—but she still didn't look very beautiful.

So Juan Bobo went to his mother's closet and got out her red taffeta skirt with the elastic waistband, and he slipped that around the pig's waist.

Then he went to the house of his great-aunt Margarita, who weighed almost three hundred pounds. He borrowed a blouse and a bright red wig, and he fit those onto the pig.

He outlined the pig's eyes as best he could with black eyeliner and a touch of blue eye shadow; he put bright red lipstick on the pig's lips; and he got two pairs of his mother's high-heeled pumps and strapped those onto her trotters.

Now the pig looked *really beautiful* to Juan Bobo! So he put a rope around her neck and started to take her to market.

But halfway along the road to town they came upon a big muddy puddle. This big muddy puddle looked *really beautiful* to the pig. She threw herself down right in the middle of the big muddy puddle, and she rolled around a couple times, because it felt so good to her.

There was nothing Juan Bobo could do about it—because she was much bigger than he was, and sometimes she just forgot that Juan Bobo was supposed to be in charge. She kicked off her high-heeled pumps—all except one that got stuck sideways. She got the red taffeta skirt all covered with mud, she ripped one sleeve out of the blouse, tore off her wig, and completely ruined her mascara.

By the time Juan Bobo got the pig out of the puddle and all the way to town, she didn't look so beautiful anymore. In fact, when the townspeople saw Juan Bobo and his pig, they laughed and laughed and laughed the two of them all the way back home.

So that today, in Puerto Rico, whenever somebody gets so dressed up that their friends almost—but not quite—don't recognize them, people say that they are "all dressed up like Juan Bobo's pig."

A WORD FROM THE WISE

The story is most effective when the teller can sink into the point of view of Juan Bobo—the total, single-minded sincerity of his efforts to beautify the pig. The two central actions—the doing and the undoing of the porcine make-over—mirror each other in each detail, and each can be given its full moment in the telling, with plenty of physicalization. After the pig's disarray is complete, the tale moves swiftly to its proverbial conclusion.

TRICKSTER TALES

Tigertail Soup

A Folktale from Jamaica

MELINDA MUNGER

Recommended audience: Ages 9 to adult.

This story comes from Jamaica. I know a couple of off-color versions, too. You see, it's not exactly Tiger's *tail* that winds up in the soup. Suffice it to say I've heard mention of two other organs, neither one of which I could mention in a school visit. But the story has a good trick in it, and I like tricks. So I bowdlerized it a bit and put in Tiger's tail. Several years later, a wonderful little picture book appeared titled *Tiger Soup* by Frances Temple that skirts the organ issue entirely. If you'd like a peek at an original version try *Afro-American Folktales,* a great collection from Pantheon edited by Roger D. Abrahams.

MELINDA MUNGER has lived in Miami, Florida, for forty-five years and has been telling stories since 1978. For eleven years she told full-time as the head of The Imagination Factory, the storytelling department of the county library system. She has appeared at festivals, fairs, schools, and conferences around Florida and the Southeast. She pulls her stories from books, of course, but also from the people around her—in grocery store lines, waiting rooms, the Metrorail, and in the schools she visits—and then tells the stories in her own way. Her goal as a storyteller is to return the stories to children whose families immigrated to America from other cultures.

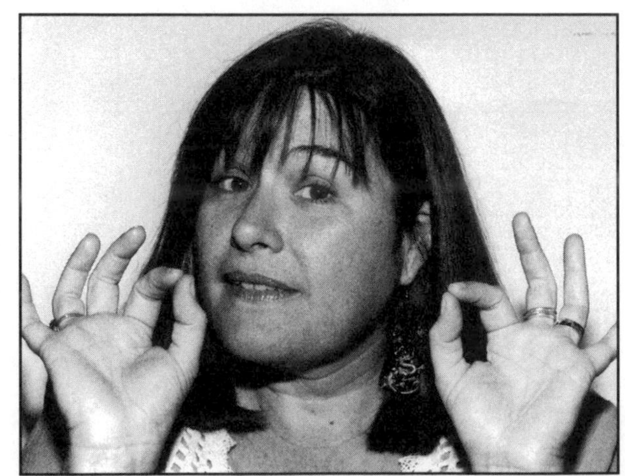

TIGERTAIL SOUP

Anansi can't ever mind his own business. One day as he was walking past the king's house, he heard the king say, "Ahh! Tigertail soup. How delicious. I love a good bowl of tigertail soup."

And Anansi thought to himself, "Tigertail soup? I have never tasted that. Huh! If it's good enough for the king, it's good enough for Anansi, too!"

So Anansi set off to fix himself a big pot of tigertail soup.

Well, you can guess the problem with making a pot of tigertail soup. Yes! Ingredients! But this wasn't a problem for Anansi. He knew where Tiger liked to swim in the morning so he headed right down to the river. Sure enough, there was Tiger relaxing in the water.

"Good morning Tiger!" Anansi hollered.

Tiger just grunted.

"How are you this morning?"

Tiger grunted again.

"Want to know a secret?"

"No!" said Tiger.

Great! Tiger was talking to him. So Anansi went on, "Sure you do. Everybody likes a good secret. Here's mine. See that place over there where the snag is sticking up? That's the best place in the whole river to swim."

Now Tiger looked more interested and swam closer. "Why?" he asked.

"Well, there's a big hole out there. The water is deeper. That means it's cooler, smoother..." said Anansi.

"Fine. Maybe it's quieter, too. I'll go swim there." Tiger started to paddle away.

"No! Wait! I didn't mean you could swim there. It's too dangerous for you."

"Why?" Tiger asked. Tigers don't like too much danger.

"Well, I told you. The water is deep out there," said Anansi.

"So?"

"Deeper water is heavier water. Big, heavy creatures like yourself try to swim in that heavy water, they sink like stones. *Especially* if they are being dragged down by big, fine, heavy tails such as yours. You ought to take that tail off and leave it up here on the riverbank. Then maybe you could swim in that nice water."

Now Tiger was proud of that tail. He didn't want to leave it *anywhere* except where it was. But Anansi pestered and pestered him and promised to watch it for him until at last—more to get some peace and quiet than anything else—Tiger popped his tail off and put it up on the bank. So Anansi paddled around in the shallow water and, as soon as Tiger stopped paying attention, he snuck out of the river, snatched up that tail and headed home.

Anansi got out his old soup pot, put in some onions, salt pork, some herbs and vegetables, and made himself a big bowl of tigertail soup. He ate it all up. It was dee-licious. Then for dessert, Anansi had... second thoughts. Anansi was *always* having second thoughts because he didn't have *first* thoughts to begin with. His second thoughts were all about what Tiger was going to do to him when he found out what Anansi had done to his tail. It was *not* going to be pretty.

Anansi came up with a few ideas for getting out of trouble with Tiger, but he didn't like any of them too much. So finally he just decided to blame the whole thing on somebody else. He headed down the road thinking of plans and looking for victims.

Before long he thought of a pretty good plan, and the very next place he came to was Big Monkey Town. Now, Big Monkeys are important people. They don't have any time for the kind of foolishness Anansi had in mind, so they just sent him down the road. But the next place Anansi came to was Little Monkey Town. Little Monkeys like to have a good time. Any excuse for a party is good enough for a Little Monkey. Anansi walked right up to the head Little Monkey of the town and said, "Hey, Chief! Guess what? I've been traveling on the other side of the island. Everybody over there is singing a new song. Want to hear it?"

Little Monkeys love new songs, so the chief said, "Sure! Sing it for me."

So Anansi starts dancing around, kicking his spider legs out, and singing this way:

Oh, yesterday
About this time,
We ate Tiger's tail up!

Yesterday,
About this time,
We ate Tiger's tail up!

Well, Little Monkey *loved* this song. He made Anansi sing it again and again. Other Little Monkeys began to gather around to learn the song, too. Pretty soon, every monkey in Little Monkey Town had voted to quit work, learn the song, sing it, dance to it, and have a great spree. As soon as the party was going good, Anansi snuck off home.

Tiger was waiting for him.

"Anansi! What have you done with my tail?"

Anansi said, "Your tail? Isn't it in its usual spot?"

"If it was, would I be asking you? You were supposed to be watching it. Where is it?"

"Oh well, Tiger, I couldn't stay by that river all day. I had to go do my errands. But, I *might* know what happened to your tail…"

"What?"

"Well, over in Little Monkey Town they are all singing a new song. Want to hear it?"

"No!" hollered Tiger, really frustrated now. *"I don't care about any stupid song. I want my tail back!"*

Anansi said, "You're going to be interested in *this* song, I bet." And Anansi started to sing the song he had taught to the Little Monkeys.

Tiger roared. He snatched Anansi up by a couple of his eight arms and legs and dragged him all the way to Little Monkey Town. Well, that party was going so good you could hear it half a mile outside Little Monkey Town. They were singing:

> Yesterday,
> About this time,
> We ate Tiger's tail up!
>
> Yesterday,
> About this time,
> We ate Tiger's tail up!

Tiger was furious! Tiger charged into that town knocking Little Monkeys left and right until he caught up to the chief. He pulled the chief right up to his nose and started demanding information about his tail.

Little Monkey didn't have any idea what Tiger was talking about and finally decided that…

"Oh! I see! You're mad because you didn't get invited to the party! Well, I'll invite you and I'll teach you this great song Anansi the Spider taught us yesterday."

Little Monkey started to sing and... Hmmmm! *Then* Little Monkey realized what was *really* going on. So did Tiger. They both turned around to find Anansi. But he was *gone*. He had run up the wall of the nearest house and hidden himself in the attic. They never did catch him.

And that's why today, if you go up in the attic and look up in the corner, you'll find Anansi. He still has to hide up there ever since that day he just *had* to taste tigertail soup.

A WORD FROM THE WISE

To tell this story, you have to know who Anansi is. In the West Indies, he is a con man—a bombastic little guy whose big mouth is always getting him in trouble. Tiger and Big Monkeys are folks who take themselves too seriously, although my feeling about Tiger is that he is more grumpy and dumb than pompous. (He is dumb in a lot of Asian folklore, too; the oppressor often is in trickster tales.)

So dig down deep: when was the last time you tried to pull a little scam? Were you a kid? Haven't you ever gotten a bit "bragadocious" yourself?

We all know folks who take themselves too seriously! And if you are lucky, there are lots of Little Monkeys in your life. Use these folks! Use your own quirks and foibles.

As for the song, make up your own tune. I did. Change the words to it a bit if you want. I did that too. Most of all, you have to have fun with it. Enjoy being the tricky one, for once. Learn it, tell it, and pass it on.

B'Whale and B'Elephant

A Folktale from the Bahamas

DEREK BURROWS

Recommended audience: I use this story with many ages and especially with young children from kindergarten to about third grade. I also use it with older children in immigrant audiences.

This is a story from the Bahamas, where I was born and grew up. This story of the tug of war is a familiar theme to many other cultures, but I heard this one in the Bahamas. B'Rabby is the Bahamian trickster. In the Bahamian style of storytelling we always use call and response to have the audience involved.

DEREK BURROWS was born and grew up in the Bahamas, where he spent summers with his grandparents on one of the islands called Long Island. They had no television or radio because there was no electricity—but they always had storytellers. He came to Boston in 1974 to study music at Berklee College of Music and has lived in Boston since then. Derek performs with a group called Voice of the Turtle, which specializes in the music of the Spanish Jews who were expelled from Spain in 1492. He began telling stories many years ago as a way of introducing his friends to Bahamian culture and customs and in order to carry on the once-strong traditions of his culture.

SUSAN WILSON

B'WHALE AND B'ELEPHANT

Once upon a time was a very old time,
the monkey chew tobacco and he spit white lime.
Wasn't my time and it wasn't your time,
it was old time
Bunday...
(audience) Bunday.

B'Rabby overheard his friends bragging about how big and strong they were. B'Rabby thought that it was time they learned a lesson. So B'Rabby got a long rope, threw it over his shoulder, and walked into the forest to find his friend B'Elephant. Now as you know this fellow B'Rabby was a pretty smart fellow. He said to B'Elephant, "Well, good mornin', B'Elephant, how you doin' this mornin'?"

B'Elephant said, "Hey there B'Rabby, I'm doin' just fine today, how 'bout you?"

B'Rabby said, "Well, B'Elephant, today I feel *strong*. In fact I feel *so* strong that I want to make a bet with you. I bet you that I can tie this end of the rope around you and pull you all the way over to the ocean."

B'Elephant laughed and said to B'Rabby, "B'Rabby, you must be kidding. Look at me—you see what a *big* fellow I am, I'm so big that even my ears are bigger than you. So tell me how you think you can pull a big fellow like me all the way to the ocean."

B'Rabby looked at B'Elephant and said to him, "Well B'Elephant, like I said, I feel *strong* today, but if you're scared to take the bet I'll go and tell everyone how you were afraid to bet with me."

"Scared?" laughed B'Elephant. "Scared? I'm not scared of anything. I'm too *big* to be scared. If you want to bet with me, fine—I'll take the bet."

"OK," said B'Rabby. "I'll tie the rope around you, and when I get to the ocean I'll blow my horn, and when you hear the horn blow start to pull."

"Go right ahead," said B'Elephant. "I'll wait to hear your signal and we'll see who is strongest."

Bunday...
(audience) Bunday.

B'Rabby took the other end of the rope and walked over to the ocean. Looking out across the ocean, he saw his friend B'Whale swimming in the ocean. B'Rabby called out to B'Whale, "B'Whale, B'Whale! It's me, B'Rabby."

When B'Whale saw his friend B'Rabby he swam in close to land. As he drew near he called out to B'Rabby, "Hey B'Rabby! How you doin' today?"

B'Rabby called back, "Well, B'Whale, I'm doing fine and I feel good too. In fact I feel *strong* today. I feel so strong that I want to make a bet with you. You see this rope? I bet if I tied this rope around you I could pull you out of the ocean and onto land."

Well B'Whale just laughed and said to B'Rabby, "B'Rabby, you see how *big* I am? I'm so big that one of my fins is bigger than you! So how can a little fellow like you pull a big fellow like me up on land?"

And B'Rabby said, "I know you are much bigger than me but I still think I can pull you up on land. However, if you're too scared to take the bet, I'll go and tell everyone that B'Whale was afraid to bet with B'Rabby."

"Me, scared?" B'Whale said. "I'm not scared of anything. I'm too *big* to be scared. If you want to bet with me, fine—I'm stronger than you and I'm sure to win this bet."

So B'Rabby tied the rope around B'Whale. "I'll take this end of the rope and go over into the forest," he said. "Listen for my signal. I'll blow my horn to let you know I'm ready to start. When you hear that sound, start to pull."

"Go right ahead," said B'Whale, "I'll wait to hear your signal and we'll see who is strongest."

Bunday...
(audience) Bunday.

B'Rabby went to the woods and climbed a tall pine tree where he could see the woods to the left of him and the ocean to the right. He had a conch shell with him with the end cut off so he could blow into it.

B'Rabby put the shell to his lips and he blew a long note. The sound of the shell could be heard far away.

Bunday...
(audience) Bunday.

B'Elephant, who heard the note first because of the direction of the wind, began to pull at the rope. But he got a big surprise. He had expected it to be easy to pull B'Rabby, but instead the rope did not budge. He said to himself, "Hmm, B'Rabby sure is strong today."

So he grabbed the rope and he pulled and he pulled and he pulled and he pulled until he pulled B'Whale right up on land.

Bunday...
(audience) Bunday.

Meanwhile, B'Whale, who was lying out in the ocean sunning himself, felt the tug of the rope and said to himself, "Hmm, B'Rabby sure is strong today."

And suddenly B'Whale found himself up on land. B'Whale looked around and when he saw that he was on land he grabbed the rope and he began to pull, and he pulled and he pulled and he pulled and he pulled until he pulled B'Elephant into the ocean.

B'Elephant found himself standing on the bottom of the ocean. He looked all around him and saw fish and turtles and all kinds of sea creatures swimming around him, and he took the rope, stepped onto land, and began to pull until he pulled B'Whale out of the water and back on land. So B'Elephant and B'Whale pulled each other back and forth from the land to the sea.

Bunday...
(audience) Bunday.

B'Rabby sat up in that pine tree and watched and laughed. He was having a great time seeing how he had fooled his friends.

Bunday...
(audience) Bunday.

Finally the rope broke, and B'Elephant landed in the middle of the woods and B'Whale landed in the ocean and B'Rabby climbed down the tree and went to find B'Elephant. When he saw him, B'Elephant said to him, "Man, B'Rabby, I didn't know you were so strong. You certainly are stronger than me. I guess you win the bet."

Then B'Rabby went to the ocean and called out to B'Whale. When B'Whale came over to him, he said, "Well B'Rabby, I didn't know you were so strong. You certainly showed me today. I guess you're the winner of this bet."

B'Rabby laughed and said, "Well my friends, next time you'll think twice about making a bet with B'Rabby."

And B'Rabby went back home feeling pleased with himself.

And they say that from that day to this, because of that tug of war, Elephant never likes going into the ocean and Whale never likes coming up on land.

e bo ben
this story done end.
Bunday…
(audience) Bunday.

A WORD FROM THE WISE

- Because call and response is part of the Bahamanian storytelling tradition, I teach the audience a call and response I learned growing up in the Bahamas. When I say the word *Bunday* (pronounced boon day), I have the audience say *Bunday* back to me. I tell the audience that when I say it, I am asking if they are listening, and when they reply, they are telling me that they are listening.

  I always start the story off with the opening rhyme included here. It is a traditional rhyme and its rhythm seems to set the mood and tone of the story. Throughout the story I use *Bunday* to keep the audience with me and it helps focus the audience. I adjust its frequency and placement depending on my audiences; younger audiences and listeners with an African or Caribbean heritage are generally more comfortable with the format.

- I first ask people if they have friends who brag about what they can do. I ask questions like, "Do you have friends who brag about how they can run faster than you, or how they can jump higher that you, or how they have more Beanie Babies than you, how they own more Microsoft stock than you [*I use this when there are parents or adults in the room*]?

  Then I say "Well, B'Rabby overheard his friends bragging about how big and strong they were and how they were stronger than anyone else, so he decided to play a trick on his friends." I try to get my listeners to recognize something familiar and something they may have in common with B'Rabby.

- The first time B'Rabby says, "I feel *strong,"* I flex my arm in a pose to show my muscle. The next time B'Rabby says the word *strong* I use the movement and have the audience fill in the word. The same is true for the word *big:* the first time Elephant says it, I use a motion with my arms out to show how big the animal is, and thereafter I use the gesture and let the audience fill in the word.

  When B'Elephant starts to pull the rope I use a pulling motion and have him pull the rope four times. I have the audience say the word *pull* each time so that they stay involved.

- When I come to the part where B'Rabby blows the horn I use a conch shell and blow into it. If you don't have one you can just say that he blew a horn. If you like, you can make a horn sound with your mouth by making an O with your lips and singing one long note.

- Sometimes, especially in schools, I tell audiences that this story was important to me as a child because when I was younger I was small and I thought that because I was small I couldn't do anything. But I learned from B'Rabby that I could be small and—if I was smart and used my brain—I could do anything. With older audiences, I talk about the tug of war as a metaphor for conflicts we feel when we are pulled back and forth in life; I share how this story reminds me of the tug I feel between the two countries I live in, the United States and the Bahamas.

- I use stories also as a part of curriculum development and you can get more information via my website: www.derekburrows.com.

Redmond O'Hanlon and the Wee Fella

A Folktale from Ireland

MAGGI KERR PEIRCE

Recommended audience: Grade 4 and up.

This is a tale about Redmond O'Hanlon. The famous highwayman once belonged to the aristocracy; in the event known as the Flight of Earls in 1609, he was banished from Ireland because of his religion, but he refused to go. This story was discovered in County Louth for the Irish Folklore Commission by Mr. Michael Murphy, a wonderful collector of folklore. I also know a song about Redmond O'Hanlon, but it has a pathetic tune, so it's better to stick to the yarn!

MAGGI KERR PEIRCE, born and reared in Belfast, Northern Ireland, has lived in Massachusetts since 1964 and been a storyteller since 1972. She has been a featured teller on many occasions at the National Storytelling Festival in Jonesborough, Tennessee, and was inducted into the National Storytelling Network's "Circle of Excellence" in 1997. Her published writing runs the gamut from folktales to memoirs, articles, and poetry. In performance, she also uses songs, rhymes and recitations from her childhood.

REDMOND O'HANLON AND THE WEE FELLA

There was this well-to-do farmer outside Dundalk who was owed a sum of money by a merchant in the town of Newry in County Down, but he had one big problem. No matter whoever he asked to go and fetch the debt, they refused him point-blank, and I'll tell you the reason why.

You see, the countryside that you had to travel through from Dundalk to Newry was well known as Redmond O'Hanlon country, and everybody thereabouts knew that they could lose their life if they met that famous highwayman and didn't give up the money.

Finally, the farmer decided he would go himself but when his wife, her name was Mary, found this out she lit into him with a few well-chosen words. "So you're not thinking of your own life," says she. "You think more of the sovereigns you're owed, and mean to leave me a widow-woman," and with that she began to weep. "Well woman," says the farmer, "who else could I ask?"

Suddenly a wee voice by the fireside pipes up—"Me, sir, I'll gladly go"—and here when they looked, wasn't there a wee fella, no more than nine years of age, no bigger than a grasshopper, putting turfs on the fire. So the farmer and the young lad began talking, and the farmer agreed that he would pay him a whole sovereign if he brought back the debt. He offered him a pistol and the fastest horse in the stable.

To the farmer's amazement the wee fella refused the pistol outright, as he had no use for firearms, nor would he take the fastest horse. Instead he asked for the oldest doddering mare to carry him, and off the boy went.

It was a lovely day and first of all the old spavined mare jogged along at a brave clip, but near to the small village the sky darkened and the countryside did not look so welcoming. The wee fella knew that he was moving into O'Hanlon country. There was not a sinner on the road for company, and he felt very much alone. Just as he came to the crossroads leading to Omeath, he heard the *clop-clop* of hooves along that road, and into view, on a magnificent chestnut filly, came riding the handsomest and best dressed man he'd ever seen. His spurs and bridle shone, his jacket was of the finest Spanish leather, his high boots gleamed, and a feather topped his hat. The servant boy had never seen anything like it in all his life. His jaw dropped as if he were catching flies.

"And where are you going on this fine morning?" asked the stranger. "Let go of your mammy's apron strings for a moment?" And with that he laughed a grand bellowing laugh. The boy was stung. This stranger didn't know how important he was.

"No such thing," the wee lad retorted. "I'm on my way to Newry to lift a debt for my master." Then he looked around at the forbidding landscape and said, "And to tell you the truth, I hear that this part of the world is Redmond O'Hanlon's country, and I'm a bit afeared."

With that, the handsome stranger let out another grand laugh and promised that on the way back he would look out for him, and no evil would befall him. And with that, he smacked the old spavined mare on the rump. "Off to Newry with you!" he shouted. And off the old horse and its young rider went, little knowing of course that the handsome gentleman was the renowned highwayman.

Well, to make a long story short, the boy found the merchant. His good lady gave the horse hay and the lad a big mug of buttermilk with a soda farl slathered in yellow salty butter fresh from the churn. The young servant had never eaten so well, and by the time he finished it, the merchant had come out of the back room with a leather pouch filled with gold coins and carefully counted out the promised amount.

"That's what the master said I should collect," said the lad, "but now I want you to take back one of those sovereigns and give me the same amount in copper coins." The merchant was puzzled, but he did what was asked. He put all the farthings, halfpennies and pennies into a big sack, and this sack the youngster carefully tied to the front of the saddle, underneath which he slipped the leather pouch.

Off they set on the road home, and never was the boy's heart lighter—his business was accomplished, and his belly full of good food. Even the old spavined mare picked up her hooves in a sprightly fashion as they bowled along the road toward Dundalk. They passed the crossroads as the sun was sinking low and were just coming up to Killevy Church when, without warning, a well-known figure on a chestnut filly sprang from behind a copse of trees. This time only his eyes were visible above a dark kerchief, but the wee lad would have recognized that hat anywhere. "Your money or your life," thundered Redmond O'Hanlon.

"B'Gob," says the wee lad, looking down the barrel of a long silver pistol, "I'm hanged if I've ever handed over money in my life, and I won't start now." With that he flung the sack that had been tied to the pommel far into the trees.

With one of those almighty roars of laughter, Redmond O'Hanlon lightly jumped off his horse. "Let nobody say that I'll not bend for mine," he said as he stepped into the wood.

As quick as a flash, the wee fella snatched the leather pouch and swung himself onto the saddle of the glorious red filly and off like the wind he raced toward Dundalk, leaving the highwayman with nothing but an old broken-down horse and a bag of copper coins.

Need I tell you that that young boy was treated like a hero when he got home? The master gave him his gold piece as promised and money besides for the lovely chestnut filly. As for Redmond O'Hanlon... well they say that he gave that part of the country a wide berth from then on, for he said if a young scamp of a fellow would trick him like that, what might the elders do?

A WORD FROM THE WISE

This is a lively tale, so tell it with vigor, as if you heard it yesterday. There is such freshness in this tale that I feel the plot itself will carry you and your listeners into the story. Make sure you make Redmond huge and loud-voiced; the boy is sly and sure of himself—as indeed he was.

How Hare Drank Boiling Water and Married the Beautiful Princess

A Folktale from Benin

RAOUF MAMA

Recommended audience: All ages.

This is a trickster tale from Benin in West Africa, a country gifted with one of the most beautiful oral traditions in Africa. This story comes out of the folktale tradition of the Fon people, the largest ethnic group in Benin today. The Fon founded in 1625 the kingdom of Dahomey, a major participant in the slave trade. Fon culture and the Fon oral tradition are shared to some extent by the black people in America, Brazil, Cuba, Haiti, and other Caribbean countries.

Here, as in many other Fon folktales, there is intermarriage between beasts and human beings. This is generally not so in western European folktales and it arguably points to a belief that beyond all the differences, there is a basic kinship between human beings and animals.

This tale is a little unusual insofar as Hare, not Yogbo the Glutton, is the trickster. But Yogbo the Glutton himself could not have done better. This story dramatizes the power of storytelling.

DR. RAOUF MAMA is an internationally known storyteller, the only one in the world today who performs in English indigenous tales from his native Benin, a French-speaking country in West Africa. Drawn from one of the richest oral traditions in Africa, Mama's stories have strong connections to African cultures on both sides of the Atlantic. He performs African and multicultural stories, blending storytelling with poetry, song, music, and dance. He gives lectures and workshops on the connection between African literature and African folklore and on the power of folktales as multicultural teaching and learning tools, especially as tools for teaching literacy skills, creative writing, and public speaking. A graduate of the University of Michigan with a Ph.D. in English, Dr. Mama is fluent in English, French, Fon, and Yoruba and proficient in Spanish and German. He teaches English at Eastern Connecticut State University and is the author of two books.

HOW HARE DRANK BOILING WATER AND MARRIED THE BEAUTIFUL PRINCESS

My story takes flight over countries and kingdoms of long ago and alights on a princess. She was famous throughout her father's realm for her flashing eyes, her smooth, glowing complexion, her flowing, jet-black hair, and her soothing voice. All who saw her were captivated by her beauty, and many dreamed of having her for their wife. When the time came at last for her to be married, a great crowd gathered as men, beasts, and birds came to ask for her hand. They all vowed to make her the happiest woman in the world, and they all clamored around as each claimed to be the bravest, the strongest, and the most handsome. The king and the princess tried very hard to listen to everyone, but it was all very bewildering, and neither of them knew whom to choose.

So, in the end, the king decided he would have to set them a challenge. He thought long and hard, and then let it be known that whoever was brave enough to drink from a pot of boiling water was the one he would allow to marry his daughter. Messengers were sent out to spread the word far and wide throughout the kingdom, and eventually the day for the contest came. A clay pot was filled with water and put on a blazing wood fire right in the middle of the royal front yard. Then the princess and the king, dressed in their finest robes, were seated in the place of honor and waited.

It was not long before the water came to a boil, sending steam rising to the sky. Soon, a big crowd gathered around, and the herald proclaimed that all those who wished to try for the hand of the princess should come forward. A prince wearing beautiful clothes of fine silk stepped out of the crowd and walked boldly toward the fire. He was tall, strong, and good-looking. A hush fell on the crowd when, using a roll of cloth to cushion his hands, he seized the clay pot from the fire and lifted it straight to his lips. For a moment it looked as though he would succeed, but a blast of heat caught him in the face, and he quickly put the pot back on the fire again and walked away, his head bowed in shame. In turn, other princes, noblemen, warriors, and hunters came forward with great bravado, but sadly they all failed, one after another, and slunk away.

Then the king of the jungle, mighty Lion, broke out of the crowd, roaring at the top of his lungs, his mane glistening in the sun. He lifted the clay pot in his rough-padded paws and brought it closer and closer to his mouth, but the heat from the steam gushing out was more than even he could bear. Whining and frowning, he, too, walked away as Eagle came circling down for his try. Eagle came as close as he could and pecked at the water, but the heat was such that he had to fly away defeated.

There followed Leopard, Elephant, Monkey, Owl, Vulture, and many more princes, chiefs, and warriors, but none was brave enough.

As the fire burned down, more wood was added and more water was poured into the pot so that it was always filled to the brim with boiling water. There was great excitement when Tortoise emerged out of the crowd. Tortoise was known throughout the land as a great diviner, and rumor had it that he could make boiling water taste fresh and cool. Turning his head now to the left, now to the right, he made straight for the blazing fire, singing:

> The fire is burning and in the pot,
> The water is steaming, boiling hot.
> I go forth to take up the challenge,
> By the power of my venerable elders,
> The distinguished fellowship of diviners,
> May I carry the day, for a change!

Rearing himself on his hind legs, Tortoise lifted the pot and raised it to his mouth. But even he, with all his magical powers, was unequal to the ordeal.

The king couldn't go back on his proclamation, and as the day wore on it began to look as though the princess would have to do without a husband. It was then that Hare broke out of the crowd and went trotting up to the fire, his ears perked up, a mischievous smile flickering about his lips. He gave a little bow to the crowd and then turned and looked thoughtfully at the pot.

The fire burned fiercely. The water boiled and bubbled, sending steam rising to the heavens. Hare took a roll of cloth to cushion his paws and then carefully lifted up the steaming pot, held it aloft, and started... talking.

First he turned to Lion and said,

> I have come to attempt what no one has done in living memory.
> I have come to drink boiling water and suffer death for my folly.
> But for every act of folly there is a reason,
> And mine is the power of love and passion.
> I beg you, O King of the Jungle—upon my passing, tell my story,
> Lest it fade from memory.

Lion agreed. In turn Hare asked Eagle, Tortoise, Monkey, Elephant, and all the other animals to tell his story, should he die after drinking the boiling water. All the animals quietly agreed, but that was not enough for Hare. He turned to the great princes, the warriors, and all the powerful people gathered there and begged them not to let his sacrifice sink into oblivion. He even spoke to the king and the princess, and each of them agreed.

Then, addressing the crowd as a whole, he concluded,

> Tell my story to your children
> And your children's children,
> Lest I die in vain.
> For when we are gone,
> Only our stories remain.

The crowd listened, enraptured by Hare's words, not realizing that the boiling water had slowly grown cold.

With the clay pot still held high, Hare bowed to the king, to the princess, and finally to the crowd. Then, he lowered the pot slowly to his lips and, with an expression of feigned agony, drank the water to the last drop. The crowd let out a great cheer as they rushed forward to acknowledge the hero. Hare had faced the terrible challenge and survived!

Hare was led to the palace with great majesty, and he and the beautiful princess were married. They lived happily together, and in time he became a great king, and they had many children, grandchildren, and great-grandchildren. To this day, the people of that kingdom still haven't realized that during all the time Hare was imploring them to immortalize his brave deed in story, he was simply waiting for the water to cool!

A WORD FROM THE WISE

Though this story works for all ages, you can adapt your language and gestures to suit the age and size of the audience. Use larger gestures and simpler wording with younger children. The story works very well for audience participation and creative dramatics. One can have many different animals, each with his or her own personality, try to drink the boiling water. The storyteller can narrate the tale while the children act it out or—if there is time—create spoken dialogue appropriate to each animal character.

The Boy and the Devil

A Folktale from the Mexican Borderland

PLEASANT DESPAIN

Recommended audience: Grades K–3.

The Mexican Borderland consists of much of southwest Texas and has contributed an abundance of folklore to our heritage. Texas produces most of the sulfur used in the United States and thus stories involving the fires of Hades and the Devil abound.

I first heard this story in 1952, at the age of nine. I struggled with reading and while on a summer visit to Fort Worth, my Uncle Henry read it to me. I know of two versions. "Satan and the Boy" is found in The Publications of the Texas Folklore Society, 1935. It was also collected in Riley Aiken's *Mexican Folktales From The Borderland* (Dallas: Southern Methodist University Press, 1980).

PLEASANT DESPAIN is recognized as one of the pioneers of America's storytelling renaissance. He's had his own television show, been featured at festivals and schools throughout the United States since the early seventies, and has 165 stories and nine books in print. Five of his books have won national awards. Having lived in Seattle and Tucson, he now calls New Hope, Pennsylvania, home.

DOMINIC OLDERSHAW

THE BOY AND THE DEVIL

Long ago there lived a bright boy who liked adventure. He ran away from home to seek his fortune and met a well-dressed stranger on the road.

"Excuse me, mister. I'm in search of a job. Perhaps you can give me some advice."

"It's possible that you can work for me," the stranger replied. "I've been looking for a helper. Can you read?"

"Oh yes," the boy responded with pride. "My mother taught me how. I read quite well."

"In that case, I won't hire you," the man said. "I need a helper who can't read."

The lad thought this was strange, but quickly responded, "You might be interested in hiring my brother. He's a good worker, but slow-witted. Mother tried to teach him to read, but he just couldn't do it. He's somewhere ahead of us on this road. Goodbye."

The boy walked away. Soon out of sight, he doubled back and ran through the woods until he was ahead of the man. He took off his colorful poncho and stepped back onto the road. The stranger walked up and greeted him.

"Are you the boy who can't read?"

"Yes, that's me."

"I'm looking for a helper to keep my house and library tidy. Do you want the job?"

"Yes, sir."

The boy moved into the stranger's house. Though it was large, it was easy to keep clean, so the lad was left with many idle hours. He began to sneak books from the library and secretly read them in his room. The books were filled with strange-sounding words and frightening drawings. It wasn't long until the boy realized that he was working for the devil himself.

Most boys would have run far away, but not this one. He was as curious as he was smart. He read several of the devil's books and learned how to change from human to animal and back again.

The devil returned home early one day and caught the boy reading. He was so angry he began to beat the lad. The boy quickly changed himself into a rat and ran away.

The devil immediately changed himself into a large cat and chased after the rat.

When the cat grabbed the rat by the neck, the boy changed himself into a dove and flew high into the air.

Not to be outdone, the devil became a hawk and soared after the dove.

Just before the hawk struck, the boy changed into a turtle and fell to the earth like a stone.

The devil, wondering what the boy was up to, thought it best to hide and watch. He changed himself into a leaf and floated gently to the ground.

The turtle crawled to the leaf and looked it over. The turtle walked around the leaf and sniffed at it. Just as the devil began to turn back into human form, the turtle opened its powerful jaws wide and chomped the leaf into tiny pieces. They were easy to swallow.

That's why, even today, the devil is wary of boys, especially the clever ones who know how to read.

A WORD FROM THE WISE

This is a great story for young boys. I take advantage of the high energy and action by physically enacting the flight and chase sequences. I also make sure to reinforce the sense of humor the story embodies.

Against the Law –OR– Br'er Wolf Still in Trouble

An African-American Folktale

JAMES "SPARKY" RUCKER

Recommended audience: All ages

In telling any of the Br'er Rabbit tales it is essential to keep a sense of humor. These stories were the only way a slave could educate his children in the ways of the world in a society where education was forbidden him by law. Slaves taught their children that no matter if their place in society was one of subservience, they could still prevail using their "brains" instead of their "brawn." Like Anansi, Jack, High John the Conqueror, Old Man Coyote, and Pandora, this trickster character could always be called upon to brighten each gloomy day.

Other variations of this tale can be found in: Joel Chandler Harris, and Richard Chase, compiler, *The Complete Tales of Uncle Remus* (Boston: Houghton Mifflin Company, 1955), pp. 315–320, tale No. 46 in *Nights With Uncle Remus: Myths and Legends of the Old Plantation* [Original Copyright, 1881]; Julius Lester, *More Tales of Uncle Remus: Further Adventures of Brer Rabbit, His Friends, Enemies, and Others* (New York: Dial Books, 1988), pp. 111–114. Julius' tale is entitled, "Brer Rabbit Saves Brer Wolf—Maybe." Julius Lester is a wonderful storyteller whose Brer Rabbit Tales are a fresh approach to these legends.

CLYDE BROADWAY

Nationally acclaimed musician and storyteller JAMES "SPARKY" RUCKER has wowed audiences throughout the United States, Canada, and Europe with his humor, witticism, and wonderful songs and stories. Rucker, formerly a teacher in Chattanooga, performs at festivals, schools, libraries, and historical sites. Sparky Rucker has appeared in such venues as the National Storytelling Festival, the Festival of Storytelling on Martha's Vineyard, and the Texas Storytelling Festival. He has also spoken or performed at the Chicago Cultural Center; the Kennedy Center for the Performing Arts; the Smithsonian; Philadelphia, Vancouver, Winnipeg, and National Folk Festivals; and several performances in Idaho honoring Martin Luther King Jr., where Rucker received the NAACP Appreciation Award. He is the author of *Tricksters From High John the Conqueror to Brer Rabbit* (Maryville: Tremont Productions, 1998).

AGAINST THE LAW –OR– BR'ER WOLF STILL IN TROUBLE

It was a *beautiful* spring day and it was a *great* day for taking a stroll. Br'er Rabbit was decked out in his usual attire…striped bib overalls [with one strap undone], red and black checkered flannel shirt, and *big* brogan shoes on his large feet. His hands were in his pockets, a sprig of straw was clenched between his teeth, and he was merrily singing an old blues tune…

> I'm a'walkin' down this track,
> got a sack on my back,
> I'm gonna make it through these woods…if I can."[1]

It was *such* a beautiful day that his heart soared with joy. His large pink-tinged ears were waving in the breeze and his pink nose twitched as he sniffed the morning air…

"Not a sign of trouble today!" he exclaimed to himself as he continued singing and loping down the long dirt road.

As he continued his sojourn, minding his *own* business [and leaving everyone *else's* alone], he heard off in the distance, a plaintive cry…

"Help me! Help me! Oh, Lordy, Lordy, somebody! Help me, please!"

Br'er Rabbit stopped, he did, and he kind of perked up his ears and tried to figure out…

"What was that?"

All of a sudden he heard it again…

"Lordy, please! Help me! Help me!"

Br'er Rabbit said, "Who is that, and where are you calling from?"

The voice responded, "Help me, please! I'm down in the gully! Come on down! Help me, please!"

Old Br'er Rabbit crawled to the edge of the road and peered down into the gully, and Lord have mercy, who'd he see? It was Br'er Wolf a'laying down there, with a devil of a big rock laying on top of him! It was just about to mash old Br'er Wolf's breath out'n his body, but it wasn't so much breath gone that he couldn't holler,

"Help me, please!"

He was hollering something fierce, and he was sounding so pitiful, that Br'er Rabbit felt sort of sorry for Br'er Wolf. He then hitched up his overalls [so they wouldn't drag and get tangled in his feet], and slid down the bank [sort of like wearing skis... with those big feet of his'n], and walked up to the boulder.

"Well... bless gracious, Br'er Wolf! How're you doing?" said Br'er Rabbit.

Br'er Wolf must have wondered why that rabbit was so dense as he said pitifully, "Br'er Rabbit, can you get this boulder off of me?"

Br'er Rabbit reckoned as if he could, but he was worried about Br'er Wolf hurting him [seeing as how Br'er Rabbit had often tricked Br'er Wolf on numerous occasions, and Br'er Wolf might be out for revenge], but Br'er Rabbit's better nature took over and he began to look around trying to figure out how he could best help Br'er Wolf.

"Well, Br'er Rabbit," pleaded Br'er Wolf, "can you hurry up and get it done? This old rock's about to mash the *breath* out of me."

Old Br'er Rabbit he *tugged*... *pushed*... and *tugged,* but... no good! He looked around *again* for something to use as a lever to help him move the rock. Poor old Br'er Wolf was starting to sound *really* pitiful now.

"Br'er Rabbit, thanks for trying to help," said Br'er Wolf, "... but could you *please* work a little *faster?*"

This started to annoy Br'er Rabbit, as he was thinking and working just as fast as he could. He finally spotted a long pole. He strategically wedged it under the boulder, and giving a mighty shove [for a rabbit], he heaved the boulder off of Br'er Wolf.

Br'er Wolf, he got up and, you know, kinda brushed himself off... and, all of a sudden, he *realized* that he wasn't as bad hurt as he'd *thought* he was. Then he come to thinking... "You know, *this* might be the time for me to get my *revenge* on Br'er Rabbit for all the tricks he done played on me."

And just as soon as he *thought* about it...his hand reached over and *snatched* Br'er Rabbit up by the nape of his neck. The *other* hand reached over and grabbed Br'er Rabbit by the seat of his britches...and he hiked him up in the air...and Br'er Rabbit went to kicking his feet, squealing and yelling,

"Lemme go! Lemme go! *Lemme go!*"

Old Br'er Wolf said, "I ain't gonna let you go...been waitin' *too long* for *this!*"

"Come on, Br'er Wolf," said Br'er Rabbit, says he. "Is *this* the way you treats somebody what's done you good? Is this the way you does someone that's helped you *out?*"

"Well," said Br'er Wolf, "I'll thanks you *now*...then makes *fresh meat* outa you *later!*"

"Well now, wait a minute Br'er Wolf," says Br'er Rabbit. "Where *I* come from it's *against the law* to *kill and eat* them what's done *helped* you!...and I *reckon* it's against the law around *here,* too!"

Br'er Wolf kinda scratched his head and thought for a while and said, "Well, I ain't so *sure* about that..."

Br'er Rabbit said, "Well why don't we go and see Br'er Terrapin[2] and let *him* decide it?"

Br'er Wolf allowed that he thought that would be OK. So off they went to see Br'er Terrapin. Upon reaching Br'er Terrapin's abode they proceeded to knock on the door...*Knock! Knock! Knock!*

An aged voice croaked behind the door, "Yes?...who *is* it?"

"It's *us,*" says Br'er Rabbit, says he. "*Me!* And Br'er Wolf!"

They could hear shuffling inside as Br'er Terrapin made his way to the door *agonizingly* slow.

Upon reaching the door he s-l-o-w-l-y opened it...There stood Br'er Terrapin dressed in a smoking jacket [which he wore *over* his shell], backless house slippers on his feet, a newspaper in his hand, and spectacles sitting on the bridge of his beak. As he peered over the top of his glasses he said,

"Morning, gents! What can I *do* for you?"

Well old Br'er Wolf told *his* side of the story...and Br'er Rabbit told *his* side of the story...and Br'er Wolf told his side *again,* and Br'er Rabbit began to tell *his* side again...when...

"Wait a minute! Wait a minute," says Br'er Terrapin, says he. "Hold it, hold it! I *believe* we're gonna have to go to the scene of where this all happened so I can figure this thing all out!"

Br'er Terrapin closed the door after going back inside, and when he next appeared he was decked out in a red vest with a gold watch and chain attached to his buttonhole, a derby hat on his noggin, and carrying a gold-headed cane to aid him in his walking.

Br'er Wolf and Br'er Rabbit looked at the immaculate Br'er Terrapin... then looked at each other and shrugged... and then they picked up Br'er Terrapin [so as not to waste time waiting for Br'er Terrapin to *walk* there... seeing as how he's so *slow*], and carried him back to the gully. They gently set him down as he asked,

"Is *this* where the dispute occurred?"

Br'er Rabbit and Br'er Wolf allowed as it was, and then Br'er Wolf loped on down into the gully. Br'er Rabbit then sat back on his heels and skied down the bank and sat beside Br'er Wolf as they waited patiently for Br'er Terrapin to come on down.

Finally they yelled up to Br'er Terrapin, "Slide down on yer back, Br'er Terrapin, slide down on yer back!"

Br'er Terrapin flipped himself over and tobogganed on down the slope. He got himself up and dusted himself off and proceeded to tap his cane to a staccato beat as he began to inspect the boulder. He walked to and fro, checking out every angle... then he wrote figures in the dirt... took off his spectacles and wiped them [setting them up on his forehead]... scratched his head... looked puzzled and said,

"I'm afraid I can't figure this thing out unless we reconstruct the situation."

"What do you *mean,*" says Br'er Wolf, says he.

"I *mean,*" says Br'er Terrapin, "that we're gonna have to put everything *back* where it was so's I can make an *estimate* of the situation."

Br'er Rabbit agreed almost *instantly*. Br'er Wolf wasn't so *sure,* but to get this thing resolved, he reluctantly agreed. He laid down, and with *much* groaning and *much* ceremony they got the boulder rolled *back* on top of Br'er Wolf. He began wheezing and said,

"Let's hurry this thing along... OK?"

Br'er Terrapin ignored him as he began to pace... back and forth... back and forth. He drew figures in the dirt *again.* He scratched his head... adjusted his spectacles... drew a few more figures in the dirt... scratched his head again, and...

"Can't you move a little *faster?*" whined Br'er Wolf as he began to look a little *more* pitiful.

Br'er Terrapin looked at him with an annoyed expression on his face, as if to say, *What'd you expect from a box turtle?*

"This old rock's a'gittin' heavy!" says Br'er Wolf, says he.

Br'er Terrapin scratched his head *again*...looked at his pocket watch... looked up in the sky with his eyes shaded and checked the angle of the sun, and drew *even more* figures in the dirt. He *then* reached into his vest pocket and pulled out a calculator, checked some *more* figures, and announced s-l-o-w-l-y...

"I've...*reached*...my...decision! Br'er Rabbit! *You* was in the *wrong!* Br'er *Wolf* was lying here...minding his *own* business when you came along and... Wasn't you on your way somewhere, Br'er Rabbit?"

Br'er Rabbit allowed as he *was.*

Br'er Terrapin continued. "Then the thing to *do* is for *you,* Br'er Rabbit, to *continue* on down the road and *stop messin'* in *other* folk's business!...and we'll *leave* Br'er Wolf *here* minding his *own* business!"

And, bless gracious, do you know what? That's *just* what they *did!*

As Br'er Rabbit strolled on down the dirt road whistling a tune, he *swore* that he could hear singing somewhere behind him...

> There's a rabbit in that log,
> and I ain't got no rabbit dog.
> Lord I *hate* to see that rabbit
> get away![3]

A WORD FROM THE WISE

Begin by explaining what "Br'er" means. My son Jamey once asked me, "Papa, why are all of these characters named Br'er?" After a side-splitting chuckle I explained to him that in African-American fundamentalist churches everyone was called either "brother" or "sister." When early writers tried to replicate the dialect they often used odd spellings to emulate southern black speech. A closer pronunciation would be *bruh,* leaving off the second syllable.

In telling this tale I like to start off by showing my audience my lucky rabbit's foot[4] as I perform this little chant:

> Brother Rabbit work your charm...
> Keep this child away from harm.

Ain't got time to kneel and pray...
Don't you *let me down* today![5]

You can use puppets in a small setting. With the addition of a neck scarf or infant overalls, the imagination will take over from there. I sometimes use my fingers instead of an actual puppet. For Br'er Rabbit, I take one hand and form my fingers into the traditional "V" for victory (or the "sixties peace sign") bending my index and long fingers slightly to resemble rabbit ears, while letting the tips of my ring and little fingers meet my thumb. This makes the nose and mouth. For Br'er Wolf I let the long and ring fingers touch my thumb, making the nose and mouth, while raising the index and little fingers for his ears.

Throughout the story I use *italics*. These are placed for emphasis when speaking those words. I also use [brackets] in the middle of a sentence. These lines should be spoken as if you are speaking confidentially to the audience. In doing Br'er Rabbit's voice when he is distressed [i.e., "Lemme go! Lemme go!"] I use a high-pitched squeal.

In singing the song you can use any tune that fits the meter.

Enjoy.

NOTES:

1 I sing these words to a tune similar to that of "Bootlegger's Blues," which was performed by the Mississippi Sheiks, a group that was popular in the 1917–1940s black music industry. This same tune has been used for many songs including "Payday."

2 Br'er Terrapin is sometimes called Br'er Box [as in "Box" Turtle]. He is also called Br'er "Cooter."

3 Adapted from the song "Payday." See previous note.

4 Harris, Complete Uncle Remus, pp. 239–246. "Brer Rabbit and His Famous Foot."

5 This chant is said by Hattie McDaniel in the movie *They Died With Their Boots On* (1941). (Ms. McDaniel was the first African-American to win an Oscar for her portrayal of "Mammy" in the movie *Gone With the Wind).*

TALL TALES

The Cherry Tree Buck

A Folktale from the Pennsylvania Mountains

ROBIN MOORE

Recommended audience: This seems to work for all ages.

From the time I was old enough to walk, my grandfather and I spent every spare moment in the woods of central Pennsylvania, enjoying whatever the wind and weather had to offer us. Here's a tale that combines my real-life memories of my grandfather with one of the oldest tales in North America, the story of the Cherry Tree Buck.

ROBIN MOORE has been a storyteller since 1981 and has presented more than three thousand programs at schools, museums, conferences, festivals, and on radio and television. Before becoming a full-time professional storyteller, Robin served as a combat soldier in Vietnam, earned a journalism degree from Penn State, and worked as a newspaper reporter and magazine editor. He is the author of the best-selling *Awakening the Hidden Storyteller* (reprinted as *Creating a Family Storytelling Tradition),* as well as three award-winning historical novels for children, *The Bread Sister of Sinking Creek, Maggie Among the Seneca,* and *Up the Frozen River.* He has also written two collections of tales from the Pennsylvania Mountains: *When the Moon is Full* and *The Cherry Tree Buck.* He is the owner of Groundhog Press, a small independent publishing house that produces books and tapes celebrating the oral tradition.

JACQUELINE MOORE

Robin Moore

THE CHERRY TREE BUCK

When I was a boy growing up in the mountains of central Pennsylvania, my grandfather used to take me deer hunting up in the woods behind our house.

We went every year in the first weeks of December, after the leaves had fallen but before the first snow, while the yellowed cornstalks still stood in the fields like a pale army rustling in the wind.

My grandfather was an old-fashioned kind of person. He never took much interest in modern hunting equipment. Year after year, all through the 1950s and 1960s, he took me hunting with the same rifle: an old flintlock muzzle-loading gun that my great-grandfather had owned many years before I was born.

In all the years we went hunting together, we had never gotten a deer. But we were never discouraged. We knew that some year something miraculous would happen.

And one year a miracle did happen. Or I guess it was a miracle. You can judge for yourself...

We set off early one morning to climb the mountainside and wait by a deer trail, hoping to catch a glimpse of a big buck.

But we were no sooner settled than we realized we had made a terrible mistake. We had the rifle and some gunpowder, but we had forgotten to bring any bullets.

We felt pretty stupid—there we were, all the way up in the woods, with no bullets.

Fortunately, my grandmother had packed us a paper bag of cherries.

We were sitting underneath a big hemlock tree, eating the cherries and spitting out the pits, when I had an inspiration. I looked down at the cherry seeds in my hand.

"Grandpa," I said, "couldn't we use these for bullets?"

My grandfather nodded. "It's sure worth a try," he said.

My grandfather dropped a charge of gunpowder down the barrel of the rifle. Then he wrapped the cherry seed in a little cloth patch and used his ramrod to shove it into the barrel. He poured a spot of priming powder in the flash pan and snapped it shut. We were ready.

Just then we heard a rustling sound up ahead, and a magnificent buck stepped out onto the trail. He was a "six-point," meaning that he had six pointed tines on each antler—a very impressive rack for a Pennsylvania deer.

My grandfather raised the rifle and sighted in on the deer's chest. He held his breath and squeezed the trigger.

There was a shower of sparks, a loud explosion—and then the air was filled with blue smoke. The rifle had gone off just fine.

But when the smoke cleared I could see the deer standing there, seemingly unhurt. He was shaking his head from side to side, as if stunned by the explosion.

I noticed that the hair on top of the deer's head was ruffled up, and I realized what had happened. My grandfather had aimed high. Instead of going into the chest, the hard cherry seed had flown through the air and stuck in the skin on top of the deer's head!

Finally, the deer came to his senses and ran off.

We both thought it was one of the strangest things we had ever seen.

The next year, in the spring, we were out walking around in that same part of the woods when we saw something even stranger.

We looked up the mountainside and there was a cherry tree in full blossom, walking down the trail toward us.

I looked and I could see: It was that deer, with a cherry tree about three feet tall growing out of the top of his head!

I realized what had happened.

That seed must have stuck under his skin all winter. In the spring some rain probably fell on him—so, naturally, the little tree just sprouted right up!

A little later in the season he got about a dozen red cherries on the tree, hanging in between his antlers.

We decided to protect the deer because, even in central Pennsylvania, we very rarely get a deer with a cherry tree growing out of the top of his head. So we posted NO HUNTING signs all over our land, and the local hunters respected that.

That deer grew up pretty well.

And the cherry tree grew pretty well, too. It got to be about fourteen feet tall. And you could get a bushel of cherries just by following the deer around and picking up what he dropped.

We had a ball watching that deer in every season.

Then one year, during the hunting season, a terrible thing happened. My grandfather and I were inside the house early one morning, eating breakfast, when we heard a sound in the woods behind our cornfield. It was the sharp, earsplitting crack of a modern rifle.

We looked out our window to see a hunter walking out of our woods and into our cornfield.

We put on our coats and walked out there to tell him he wasn't allowed to be on our land. But as we were walking through the dried cornstalks we saw something dark lying in the cornrows.

When we got closer, I could see it was the cherry tree buck.

I never saw my grandfather lose his temper like he did that day. He stormed through the dried corn and located the hunter just as he was coming to the edge of the fields. I could see that he wasn't from around here; he was one of those sportsmen who drive up from the cities every fall with the price tags still hanging from their hunting clothes. My grandfather grabbed him by the scruff of his neck and the seat of his pants and walked him off our land.

When he came back, my grandfather examined the deer. But it was no use.

The deer was dead.

Normally, when we came across a road kill or when someone gave us a deer he had shot and didn't want, we would give the meat to my grandmother and she would use it for steaks and soups and stews. My grandfather would tan the skin for moccasins and hunting bags. And we would find a use for just about every part of the deer: tying fishing flies from the tailhairs and making whistles from the legbones.

But we didn't do that this time. Instead my grandfather got two shovels from his workshed. We dug a hole in the center of the cornfield and buried the deer with his legs folded under him, his nose facing west, and that cherry tree sticking up out of the ground.

It was worth a try.

The following spring the tree gave us a beautiful crop of cherries.

Early in the season, I walked out with my stepladder and bucket to pick the first cherries of the year. I set up my ladder and climbed into the upper branches, dropping the cherries into my bucket.

Then I made the mistake of popping one into my mouth.

"Ow!" I yelled. I had bitten into something sharp.

My grandfather came running over. "What's the problem?" he asked.

I fished around in my mouth and pulled out two little twiggy-looking things.

"I'm all right, Grandpa. I must have gotten a sharp stem in my mouth," I said.

I reached up, picked another cherry, and slipped it in my mouth.

"Ow!" I hollered again. That hurt worse than the first time!

"Now what?" my grandfather said. "Is there something wrong with those cherries?"

Something had jabbed into my tongue. I reached into my mouth and pulled out two sharp curvy things.

Then I looked up into the cherry tree and realized what had happened: every one of those little individual cherries had a tiny set of deer antlers in them!

"Well, I'll be—" my grandpa said. "That's amazing."

It *was* amazing. Year after year that tree bore us crops of cherries with little six-pointers in them. They were perfectly good cherries. The only problem was, by the time you had de-pitted and de-antlered them, it would take you all afternoon to get enough for a pie.

We still have a few of those miniature antlers around the house. We use them for toothpicks when company comes over.

As far as I know, that cherry tree is still growing in the center of our cornfield. And I hope it grows there a long, long time.

A WORD FROM THE WISE

I always start tall tales by telling something which is truthful. For instance, I like to say something about my grandfather, being sure to add some actual details about the things he and I did when I was a boy. I start with a reasonable premise (forgetting the bullets) then move on to a fairly reasonable solution (why not use the cherry pits?) until the tale takes on a life of its own. I used to end the tale with the cherry tree growing in the center of the cornfield—then one day I spontaneously added the antlers. This sudden inspiration added one more twist to the tale.

Once, when I was telling stories at a school in rural Pennsylvania, the kids surprised me by giving me a realistic wooden replica of a cherry—complete with delicately carved wooden antlers! (I use it as a prop now—just in case there are any disbelievers.) Their teacher mentioned that they used to have Cherry Tree Bucks in northern Pennsylvania when she was a girl but that they are nearly extinct now. She claimed her mother devised a clever way to simplify the de-antlering step: She would put the cherries in a jar, cover them with syrup-water and let them sit on a shelf until the hunting season was over and the deer drop their antlers. Once the antlers settled to the bottom of the jar, she would strain the contents through cheesecloth and sort out the cherries and the toothpicks!

The Talking Dog

A Folktale from the Southern Mountains

DOC McCONNELL

Recommended audience: Adults and mature teens.

This tale has been around forever and has been told in many versions. Set in hard-working rural America, the story concerns a lazy young man who hoodwinks his naïve and loving father and then devises a plan to cover up his drastic deeds. My version is "fair game" for all who want to retell it.

Although DOC McCONNELL is a Southern storyteller with a mountain flavor, he provides a fresh look at storytelling as part of American life and everyday events. He is the barker of his own Doc McConnell's Old-Time Medicine Show. He was born near Tucker's Knob, a small farm community near Rogersville, Tennessee. He is a favorite at festivals, fairs, conventions, schools and libraries throughout the United States. He has appeared on "A Prairie Home Companion," "CBS Morning News," "Hee Haw," "Today," "Real People," and many other programs.

THE TALKING DOG

Uncle Nemo didn't live in town. He and Cousin Bo lived over across the river in the country. Uncle Nemo was a good old man and worked hard at his trade as a tile setter and linoleum layer. He wanted the best for his family, which consisted only of Cousin Bo and Bo's bulldog, Ace.

Cousin Bo never was very inclined to work and spent most of his time trying to get out of work. He was smart enough to work, but his mind seemed to look for ways to keep from working. Though he never did very well in school because of his laziness, he somehow seemed to get by year after year without having to repeat a grade. It was mostly because he would cheat on his papers and even went so far to steal blank report cards out of the school office and make up his own grades to take home to Uncle Nemo.

Uncle Nemo wanted Cousin Bo to do well and urged him to work hard, but the advice fell on deaf ears. Cousin Bo somehow edged through grammar school and, by the skin of his teeth, finished high school there at Rockville. It was a surprise to most who knew Cousin Bo that he even finished school at all since he had spent most of his time loafing around and riding the ferry-boat that crossed the river, hanging around during school hours at Bill Sprankle's store or the gas station.

It was one of Uncle Nemo's dreams that his boy, Cousin Bo, would go to college. After high school, Uncle Nemo made Cousin Bo apply for admission to the State Teachers College in the state capital. By mid-summer, they were notified that Cousin Bo was accepted for classes at the college. Uncle Nemo started getting the money together for Cousin Bo to go off to school. He knew better than to send all the money at one time with Cousin Bo. He gave him only the immediate funds necessary to see him through the first part of the year and kept the remainder for later expenses.

Cousin Bo did not want to go off to college, and to try to keep from going he demanded that he take his favorite dog, Ace, with him. He told Uncle Nemo that he just couldn't bear to leave his dog at home. Cousin Bo thought that this would cause Uncle Nemo to not send him off to college. But Uncle Nemo was so determined that Cousin Bo go to college that he agreed that the bulldog, Ace, could go along with Cousin Bo to the state capital to college.

In the early fall, Cousin Bo packed his clothes and the college money, put Ace on his leash, and caught the bus for college. The bus driver was about to not let the bulldog on the bus there in Rockville, but Uncle Nemo convinced him that the boy wouldn't go to college without his favorite bulldog.

Cousin Bo arrived at college and got settled. It wasn't long before he began to fall behind in his studies. He began spending more and more time with the girls, visiting the nightspots, spending his money, and missing most of his classes. He was having a good time and decided that going off to college wasn't such a bad idea after all.

Cousin Bo's money was soon gone and the school term was just getting underway. He needed more money because he was spending it on girls, nightlife, and fun. He was so desperate that he took his dog, Ace, over to a dog dealer and sold him for fifty dollars. Soon that money was gone, too.

In desperation, Cousin Bo wrote Uncle Nemo a letter. He reported that the college had made an astonishing discovery and a strange thing had happened. He went on to explain that his bulldog, Ace, being exposed to college life and the educational process, was learning to talk. He explained that the professors had taken an interest in Ace and were giving him private instructions. Cousin Bo claimed that the college professors had tested the dog and that Ace was found to have a good mind and was very bright. They felt that if Ace would enter college and begin taking classes, he could become a brilliant student.

The hitch was that the college required money for Ace. Cousin Bo claimed that there was no doubt that if these fees and expenses were paid, Ace would become the smartest dog in the world and he would begin making lots of money on exhibitions and lecture tours. People would pay a lot of money to see the world's only talking dog.

Uncle Nemo read Cousin Bo's letter and sent more money. The money was soon spent and Cousin Bo was still not doing well in school. He was spending more and more time outside of class. He now needed to write home and report on the bulldog's educational progress, as well as his own, and ask for more money.

Cousin Bo wrote home to Uncle Nemo that he was doing well and that Ace, the world's only talking bulldog, was completing his courses in record time. He went on to explain that the professors noted Ace's special talent with languages and recommended that he take some foreign languages like Greek or Latin. He told Uncle Nemo that it looked like the dog would graduate in only one year and would very soon be on the road making big money on exhibits and lectures across the country. Uncle Nemo believed Cousin Bo again and sent him more money.

At the end of the school year, Cousin Bo wrote Uncle Nemo that he was coming home. On the designated day, Cousin Bo rode the bus home to Rockville and crossed the river and headed home. Uncle Nemo saw him coming and ran down the road to meet him. He proudly embraced Cousin Bo because he was so glad that his boy had gone off to college and, on top of all that, they now had a college-educated talking dog.

Uncle Nemo stepped back and looked around. He didn't see Ace, the world's only college-educated talking bulldog. He asked where the dog was, for he wanted to hear the dog talk and especially wanted to hear him talk in a foreign tongue. But the dog was nowhere to be seen.

Again Uncle Nemo asked where the dog was. Cousin Bo stammered and stuttered and kicked the gravel in the road. Finally he answered.

"You see, Daddy, that bulldog really did learn to talk—the best I ever heard anybody talk. I was looking forward to showing him to you and letting him make you a lot of money in show business, but something happened on the way home. You see, that dog sure did learn to talk, and he was getting to where he was talking too much. We was crossing on the ferryboat from over in Rockville where we got off the bus. Well, that dog got to talking. In fact, he got to talking real big. He got to talking and telling lies about you and the hired girl in the workshop. I was just not going to have him coming home and going around the neighborhood telling lies about you, so I just kicked that rascal right off the ferryboat into the river. You know that lying bulldog couldn't swim and drowned."

Cousin Bo never went back to college.

A WORD FROM THE WISE

The story is told as a conflict between a father who wants the best for his son, and a son who prefers fun to a good education. A feeling of good intent is reflected in the beginning, as the father excuses the son for his faults and pacifies him by letting him take his dog to college. The story changes to the point of view of the boy who spends all the money and then schemes to stay on at college in order to get more money. This tension sets up the humor nicely, so that you can remain dry and impartial in your telling. But you can certainly allow yourself a faint devilish grin every time the boy outwits his father.

The Snake and the Frog

An Adaptation of a North American Fishing Tale

JON SPELMAN

Recommended Audience: All ages.

This is a bare-bones version of my adaptation of an old tall tale. As I have told this story over the years, it has grown to be at least ten, more often fifteen, minutes long. Tall tales work best when they are grounded (or at least *seem* to be grounded) in everyday, acceptable facts, so I spend a lot of time talking about Council—describing our relationship, talking about how we like to fish together, about how we are always challenging each other to friendly bets, even describing how Council has a tendency to talk too loudly. I also am careful to set up the details of this particular fishing trip, and I frequently set the tale in a location familiar to my particular audience for that telling, and describe how we came to be fishing at some distance from each other, standing at the water's edge. I allow the exaggerations and repetitions of the phrase "seven or eight" to provide a few clues that this is a tall tale, but otherwise I try to keep the details realistic, if a bit comical.

JON SPELMAN has been a storyteller, writer, and collector of stories since the 1980s. He has represented the American storytelling community at The Colloquium on the Revival of Storytelling held in Paris and was the first American to perform at the International Festival of Solo Theatre Performers in Tel Aviv. He has received a Children's Radio Award, a Parents' Choice Gold Award, an Achievement in

Children's Television Award and two Emmy Awards. Spelman is married to choreographer Liz Lerman; they live with their daughter Anna Clare in Silver Spring, Maryland.

THE SNAKE AND THE FROG

One day, I went fishing with a friend of mine—his name is Council Register—and Council and I were standing on the bank of a little river about one hundred feet apart, when I heard an unusual gurgling, bubbling noise. I looked down into the river. About seventeen or eighteen feet away from me was a large, flat rock; it was as flat and smooth as a large table, about seven or eight feet long, and only about an inch above the surface of the water. Up on that rock was the biggest frog I've ever seen, water still running off his back. This frog was enormous—it must have weighed seven or eight pounds. I put down my fishing pole and walked as quickly and quietly as I could upstream to where Council was fishing.

"Council, Council," I whispered, "come and look at what I found. I bet it's the biggest frog you ever saw."

"Naw," he said, "naw. We've got 'em really big where I come from."

"Not this big," I said.

"Put your money where your mouth is," he said.

"Fifty cents," I said, and he agreed. We tiptoed downstream, and I pointed out the frog to Council.

"Golleee!" he said. "That *is* the biggest frog I ever saw."

But before I could even ask for my money, we heard another sound from the water by the rock, a kind of a big *blip*. Coming up onto the rock, behind the frog, where the frog couldn't see it, was a snake. It was some kind of big water snake, almost as thick as my wrist, and really long—probably seven or eight feet long. The snake had started to slither up onto the rock, probably to get some sun, but when he saw the frog, he stopped. He just froze in place; only his tongue moved in and out. Keeping his head up and his eyes fixed on the frog's back, that snake started to slowly coil up onto the rock, getting ready to strike.

"Oh, Council," I said, "too bad, that snake is gonna eat that frog."

"You city boys don't know nothin'. You see the size of that frog? That frog is gonna eat that snake."

"Listen," I said, "I may live in Washington D.C., but I'm not a *total* idiot. Frogs don't eat snakes; snakes eat frogs."

"Not that frog, not that snake."

"How much do you wanna bet?"

"Fifty dollars," said Council.

"Twenty-five," I said.

"Twenty-five fifty," he said, and I agreed.

I was sure I was going to win. That big snake opened up his mouth real wide, leapt forward, and grabbed the frog by its back side and started to swallow it. Snakes don't chew things, you know, they swallow them whole; so there was the frog, going rear-end first, down the snake's throat.

"Council," I said, "pay me."

And he was actually reaching for his wallet when all of a sudden, something else happened. The frog, naturally, had been trying to get away, thrashing about, trying to turn around on the rock; and, quick as a wink, things changed. The snake's tail flipped right in front of the frog's mouth, and all of a sudden, the frog grabbed the snake's tail in his mouth, and the frog started to eat the snake. But, at the other end, the snake was still eating the frog. There they were, eating each other. And they were not polite eaters either, swallowing large gulps, making big slurping noises.

It was really exciting—it wasn't clear which one was going to win by eating the other one first—first the frog would get ahead, then the snake, then the frog again. Council and I got so wound up, we doubled the bet, to fifty-one dollars, and later, I would have tripled it, because, finally, right near the end, they seemed dead even. Only about a half-inch of the snake was left, and just the frog's lips were still visible. And then, all of a sudden, they both took a big bite—at exactly the same moment.

And they were gone. Swallowed each other right up, and we never saw either one of them again.

A WORD FROM THE WISE

Sometimes, for adult audiences, I add a bit more to the end of the tale:

> "Hey," said Council, "the frog ate the snake; you owe me fifty-one dollars."
> "Yeah," I said, "but the snake ate the frog; you owe me fifty-one dollars."
> "All right," said Council, "let's pay up."
> So we each gave the other one fifty-one dollars; and that night I heard

Council bragging to someone about how he had won more than fifty dollars from me because I didn't know anything about animals.

For audiences of children, I may add:

"Isn't that amazing? Hard to believe, even? In fact, when I told my wife about it the other night, she didn't believe me. She said I was lying. But you don't think I'm lying, do you?"

And that provides an opportunity for us to discuss tall tales and how they work.

HOW AND WHY TALES

Tía Miseria

A Folktale from Portugal

HARLYNNE GEISLER

Recommended audience: Grade 4 through senior adults.

I heard storyteller and friend Olga Loya tell the Puerto Rican version of "Tía Miseria" at a concert. I loved the story, but didn't even think about telling it for a couple of years because it was a signature story of Olga's. Finally, the story wouldn't go away, so I began to research different versions. I found the Puerto Rican tale in *Greedy Mariani and Other Folktales of the Antilles* by Dorothy Carter. I didn't like the Haitian version in *The Singing Turtle and Other Tales from Haiti* by Philippe Thoby-Marcelin because the word "miseria" was translated as "poverty." At the time I bristled at the suggestion that poverty couldn't be cured. It was the Portuguese version in *The Little Horse of Seven Colors and Other Portuguese Folk Tales* by Patricia Lowe that seemed closest to my vision of this story. You can find Olga's Spanish and English versions in her book, *Momentos Mágicos/Magic Moments.*

I told this story about misery at a clown concert at the 1988 Laugh Makers conference. It was a strange moment. Clowns cavorted across the stage; after they ran backstage, I came out and told this tale. Then the clowns continued their romp. The next morning the pantomime teacher came up to tell me how astounding she considered the story. "Look," she said, pulling up her sleeve, "even just talking about it makes goosebumps go up my arm."

While this story is funny and enjoyable to tell, it has a sting in the tail.

HARLYNNE GEISLER has been a professional freelance storyteller since 1980. She draws on her Irish and Scottish background to tell Celtic tales, and her programs range from "Hauntingly True Ghost Stories" to "Riddle Me This: Puzzling Tales" to "Woof! Dog Tales Around the World." She is an artist with the Orange County Performing Arts Center's artist-in-the-schools program in California but performs for children and families nationwide. She edits *Story Bag: A National Storytelling Newsletter* and wrote the award-winning book *Storytelling Professionally: The Nuts and Bolts of a Working Performer*. Every month she changes the listing of national storytelling events and the Short, Short Story on her website at www.swiftsite.com/storyteller. She lives in San Diego but performs in her home state of Illinois four times a year.

TÍA MISERIA

Tía Miseria was an old, old, old woman, and Tía Miseria lived in a little house with a small garden in which there grew one pear tree. The children in her town loved pears, and if they had asked Tía politely, she would have been happy to give them a few. But no, they would sneak into her garden, climb up into her tree, and steal her pears! When Tía saw them, she would hobble out and shake her fist at them. They knew that she couldn't climb the tree, so they would laugh and mock her, calling, "Tía Miseria! Neh, neh, neh!"

Tía couldn't chase them. She couldn't get their parents to do anything about it, either. But she thought about it all the time.

If you were polite, Tía was always willing to share. One day an old man, bent with years and covered with the dust of the road, stopped by her door and asked if he might rest for a moment on her chair, if he could have a drink of water. Tía saw how tired and hungry he looked. "You must eat half of my supper and take my bed tonight. I can sleep on the floor."

In the morning, the old man went to the door and turned to thank her. As he did, he stood up straighter and taller, and the years fell from him like rainwater.

"Tía Miseria, you have been kind, and for your kindness I would grant you a wish—anything you like."

Tía Miseria knew what she wanted! She took the stranger out to her tree. "Anyone who climbs my tree should be stuck there until I say they can come down."

It was a strange request, but the stranger said, "It shall be so," and he vanished.

The next day the children crept into her garden and began to grab her pears. Tía came out and watched them. They mocked her. "Tía Miseria! Neh, neh, neh!" She just smiled.

When they had eaten their fill, the children tried to leave but found they couldn't move. All those little bottoms stuck to the long thin branches.

The children wept, and they begged, but Tía just said, "Neh, neh, neh!" Finally, when they promised never again to steal a pear, Tía snapped her fingers. They came down out of the tree and were gone in an instant.

Now as I said, Tía Miseria was an old, old, old woman, and one day Death came knocking at her door. Tía answered and said, "Oh, is it time already? Well, if I must go, I must go, but first do me a favor. Pick me a pear."

Death climbed up into her tree, plucked a piece, and found himself stuck fast! Oh, he roared, and he threatened. But Tía just replied, "Neh, neh, neh!" It's not many of us who can thumb our noses at Death!

The days went by, and the weeks, and the years, but no one died, for Death was caught in Tía Miseria's pear tree.

One day her neighbor came to see her. "Tía, I am an old woman. I can't open my hands because of the arthritis, and my knees ache all the time, and I do not sleep at night. Please, Tía, let Death go, because I am ready to go with him."

Since the neighbor asked politely, Tía released Death... but not before getting a promise that he would never come for her.

So Death comes for us all, but Tía Miseria lives on, which is why we will always have miseria—misery—in the world.

A WORD FROM THE WISE

Before you tell this story, explain to the listeners that "tía" means "aunt." Don't translate the word "miseria" until the end of the story.

In the two instances in which I refer to Tía Miseria as an old, old, old woman, be sure to pause after each "old" to emphasize her age. When you say, "Neh, neh, neh!," put your open hand in front of your nose, with your thumb almost touching your nose, and open and close your hand with a mocking look on your face. When you do the gesture as the children, look down as if staring at Tía. When you do the gesture as Tía, look up as if seeing someone in a tree.

Grandmother Spider Brings the Light

A Folktale from the Kiowa People of North America

SHERRY NORFOLK

Recommended audience: PreK and grades K–2.

As a resident artist with the Alabama Arts Council, I was asked to teach first graders to tell a Native American story from the Southeast. This version of a Cherokee/Creek/Kiowa *pourqoui* tale was developed especially for that assignment—it's a simple telling that maintains the bones of the story while shedding a lot of the details. The very stylized gestures help very young children remember and retell the story. They help kinetic and visual learners grasp the story sequence, and provide visual cues which aid in retention.

With a B.A. in Elementary Education and a master's degree in Library Science, SHERRY NORFOLK performs and teaches in storytelling residencies throughout the mid-South. In her career as a children's librarian, she found that storytelling was an effective means of motivating children to read, and her years in the classroom taught her the power of storytelling as a non-didactic way to teach universal values. Sherry and her husband Bobby Norfolk are the authors of *The Moral of the Story*.

JAMES VISSER PHOTOGRAPHY

GRANDMOTHER SPIDER BRINGS THE LIGHT

In the beginning, there was darkness, darkness, darkness.

Using your arms like windshield wipers, swipe your right arm across your body on the first "darkness," your left arm on the second, and your right again on third.

The animals couldn't see where they were going, and they were always bumping into each other!

"Ouch! Stop that! Get off my tail!"

Jerk, bump, push, and shove at imaginary critters.

So they called a great council of all of the animals, and tried to decide what to do.

Describe a huge imaginary circle with your arms.

"We need light!" said Rabbit. "We can't see a thing in this darkness."

"That's right," the other animals said. "We need light. But where do we get it?"

"Well, when there is a thunderstorm, I sometimes see a crack in the sky, and light shines through. I figure if we send someone to the crack in the sky, he can bring back some light and then we can see!" answered Rabbit.

"Great idea!" they all said. "Who will go? Who will go get light?"

Hold your hands, palms up, waist-high at either side of your body.

"I'll go," said Buzzard. "I will go get light."

Buzzard was big and tough, with long, strong wings, so the others agreed.

Spread and flap your "wings," keeping elbows just slightly bent and moving mostly from the shoulders. (Buzzard is pretty dumb, so try to look goofy as well!)

Buzzard spread his long, strong wings and started off toward the crack in the sky.

Keep flapping!

When he got there, he broke off some of the light.

Reach far to your right and pretend to break off a handful of light.

"Hmmm. Now how am I going to carry this light back to the other animals?" thought Buzzard.

Look around…

"Oh! I know! I have all of these thick, beautiful soft feathers on my head. I will make a nest of the feathers to carry back the light!"

Point proudly to your head

And he put the light on his head.

Put the ball of light on your head.

Now Buzzard didn't know about light—he didn't know that it was made of fire. He didn't know that it would burn through the feathers on his head.

So he started flying back, flapping his long, strong wings.

Flap again…

Suddenly, the light began to burn through the feathers. It burned his head.

"Oooouch!" yelled Buzzard. He rubbed his head.

Jump in surprise and rub hard!

The light had burned all of the feathers off of his head! He was *bald!*

And the light had burned out.

There was darkness, darkness, darkness.

Repeat windshield-wiper motion.

"Who will go? Who will go get light?"

Repeat shrugging motion.

"I will go," said Possum. "I will go get light."

Hold your forearms close to your chest, making claws of your hands and "trotting" them slightly.

Possum started out, heading for the crack in the sky.

Keep trotting...

She broke off a piece of the light.

Reach far to the right and break off a handful of light.

"Now, what will I do with this light? I know! I'll be smarter than Buzzard. I won't put it on my head. I'll put it in my nice, bushy tail!"

So Possum put the light in her tail, and she started back.

Put ball of light on "tail" with proud look.

Suddenly, the light burned through the hair on her tail.

"Ooowwww!" yelled Possum. She looked at her tail. The light had burned all of the hair clean off—her tail was *naked!*

Jump and rub hard!

And the light had burned out.

There was darkness, darkness, darkness.

Repeat windshield-wiper motion.

"Who will go? Who will go get light?"

Repeat shrugging motion.

"I will go," said a tiny voice.

Wiggle fingers of one hand, spider-style.

"Who's that? It's too dark to see. Who's talking?"

Look around in all directions.

"It's me, Grandmother Spider. I will go get light."

Wiggle spider-hand.

"You're too small. And you're too old. You'll get lost and forget your way back. You can't go!"

"Well, I may be little and I may be old, but I think you ought to let me try."

Wiggle spider-hand.

"Let her try!" the animals said.

Nod head vigorously.

So Grandmother Spider started off toward the crack in the sky. She knew that she might forget her way back, so she spun a web all the way from where the animals were waiting, across the sky to the light.

"Walk" the (right) spider-hand across your body toward the light, meanwhile following it with the index-finger of your left hand pointing down, indicating the thread.

When she got the light, she remembered what had happened to Possum and to Buzzard.

So she scooped up some cool, wet mud, and she placed the light into the mud so that she wouldn't burn herself.

Hold light in right hand while scooping up a handful of mud with the left.

Then, she started back, following the web back to where the animals waited.

Cradle light in right hand and follow the down-pointing index-finger of left hand back.

On the way, the light baked the mud until it was dry and hard. It was the first bowl in the world!

When Grandmother Spider got back to the animals, she flung the ball of light into the sky!

Fling right arm into the air, releasing the light and spreading fingers of upheld right hand wide.

Now, ever since that time, Buzzard has had a bald head.

Flap arms, then rub head.

Possum has had a naked tail.

Make claws, then rub your behind.

Spider's web has been shaped like the rays of the sun.

Hold hands close together, spreading fingers wide like the rays of the sun.

And there has been LIGHT!

On the word "light," fling both arms high in the air with fingers spread wide.

A WORD FROM THE WISE

After telling the story once, ask the kids to help retell it "with *no* words"—just using the gestures while *thinking* the words. Total silence and concentration ensue as the whole group mimes and visualizes the story!

How the Rabbit Lost Its Tail

A Folktale from Haiti

LEN CABRAL

Recommended audience: Grades K–5.

This Haitian tale is a variation of a "how and why" story told in many countries around the world. "How and why" tales were devised to explain events that were not understood. This version contains both individual and group participation.

LEN CABRAL is a nationally acclaimed, award-winning storyteller and author who has been enchanting audiences since 1976. Len's strong Cape Verdean ancestry comes alive in his retelling of African, Caribbean, and Cape Verdean folktales. The author of a children's book for young readers as well as *Len Cabral's Storytelling Book,* Len also has four audiocassettes that have won such awards as the NAPPA Gold and Parents' Choice Silver Honor. He makes his home in Rhode Island (with his wife and two teenage daughters) and was recently honored as one of Rhode Island's Remarkable People.

JOHN MEYERS

HOW THE RABBIT LOST ITS TAIL

Long ago,[1] and this was a long time ago, rabbits had very, very long tails. This was when stones were soft and some animals were not quite ready yet. This was the time when the rabbit and the dog were best of friends. In those days, the rabbit and the dog were always together, just like best friends today. They would have breakfast together, lunch together, and dinner together.

One morning when the rabbit and the dog were having breakfast together and chatting quietly, like best friends do, Anansi came by. Now, Anansi was rather jealous of the friendship between the rabbit and the dog.[2]

Well, the dog saw Anansi first, and said, "Anansi, what are you doing up so early? You never get up before twelve o'clock."

"I got up early this morning, you see, because there's a boat leaving and it's going to the magical island."

"The magical island? I always wanted to go the magical island," said the dog.

"Well, you can't go."

"Why not?"

"You don't have any horns. The only animals allowed on the boat are animals with horns, so you can't go."

"But I want to go on the boat. I want to go on the boat; I want to go on the boooat," said the dog.

"You can't go. You don't have any horns."

The dog looked at the rabbit and said, "I want to go on the boat; I want to go on the boat; I want to go on the boooat."

The rabbit said, "You heard what Anansi said. We don't have any horns, so we can't get on the boat."

Anansi knew he had planted the seeds of trouble. He turned and went into the woods to his home.

"I want to go on the boooat," said the dog.

"Well, let me think," said the rabbit. "Oh, I have an idea. Let's go into the woods and each get two long sticks and a couple of leaves. We'll poke the sticks up through the leaves, and we'll get some vines and tie the sticks together like headpieces, like bonnets. And once we place them on our heads, we'll look just as if we have horns."[3]

And that's just what they did. They went into the woods and each found two long sticks, and they each got a couple of leaves, and they poked the sticks up through the leaves, and they got some vines and they tied the sticks into headpieces—like bonnets. Now the headpieces were rather heavy, so they had to help each other place them on their heads.

So the dog said, "Rabbit, you help me put mine on, and I'll help you with yours."

The rabbit agreed. He picked up a headpiece and placed it on the dog's head.

The dog then tied a nice bow under his chin and walked over to the water to look at his reflection. With those sticks pointing up in the air it made him look just as if he had horns. He said, "I look nice; I look nice; I look niiice."

The rabbit said, "Yeah, you look nice. Now help me put mine on."

"Wait a minute, I'm looking at myself. I look nice; I look nice; I look niiice."

"Will you help me?" said the rabbit.

Just then, they heard a horn blow. The boat was pulling anchor. The dog said, "Oh, I gotta go. Goodbye." And off he went.

The rabbit said, "But wait, but wait, but wait for meeeee."

The dog ran and he got right in line with all those animals with horns[4]—a cow, a rhinoceros, a yak, a giraffe, a wildebeest, an antelope, a gazelle, a buffalo, a bison, a unicorn, a moose. All those animals with horns were getting right on the boat, and the dog with his phony horns, he got on the boat, too.

When the rabbit saw this, he was angry. The boat started to sail away. The rabbit noticed a little hill next to the water, and he quickly ran over and climbed to the top of that hill.

As the boat was sailing by, the rabbit called out, "Captain! Oh, Captain! One of your passengers has no horns."

Hearing this, the dog ran over to the captain. "Captain, did you hear what he said? He said, turn the boat to the left, to the left."

So the captain, he turned that boat to the left.

The rabbit ran over to the next hill and called out, "Captain! Oh, Captain! One of your passengers has no horns."

Once again the dog went over to the captain, and said, "Captain, did you hear what he said? He said, turn the boat to the right, to the right."

So the captain turned the boat to the right.

The rabbit looked ahead and saw only one hill left. He ran over to the top of that hill and called out in a mighty voice[5]... "Captain! Oh, Captain! One of your passengers has no horns."

The wind took those words across the water, over the stern of the boat, right up to the captain's ears. "One of my passengers has no horns?" the captain exclaimed. "Trim the sail, drop the anchor, stop the boat—and line up!"

All the animals lined up, and the captain walked over to the cow and checked her horns. Then he checked the moose, and the wildebeest, the yak, the ox, the unicorn, the giraffe, the rhinoceros, the antelope, the elk...He was getting closer and closer to the dog. The dog knew he was going to get caught, so he jumped over the side of the boat, and he started doing the doggy paddle.[6]

When the rabbit saw the redness in the dog's eyes, he lit on out. As he ran, his long tail flopped...and he ran, and his long tail flopped...and the dog was still doing the doggy paddle until he reached the sandy beach. He shook himself dry, and then he lit out after that rabbit. While the rabbit ran, his long tail flopped, and the dog was gaining. The rabbit ran, his long tail flopped, and the dog was gaining...and gaining...and gaining...

Finally, the rabbit reached the safety of his home, and he jumped down that rabbit hole. But, he didn't have enough time to pull down that long, bushy, beautiful tail. The dog came up right behind him, and he bit that rabbit's tail right off. And ever since that day, rabbits have short little tails...and dogs are always chasing them.

A WORD FROM THE WISE

The points below elaborate on specific lines in the story that are referenced with corresponding numbers:

1. I often start the story with the question, "Do rabbits have long or short tails?" This question immediately draws in the audience members. "Short!" they invariably respond. When I tell them, "Well, *now* they do," they really focus their attention and become visibly eager to learn more about the end of long-tailed rabbits.

2. Here I interject, "Nobody here is jealous, right?" Usually I'll be answered with laughter; if there's not much response, I may say, "Oh, good, I'm glad." Either way, the audience stays with me.

3. I usually pause before I say the last word in this sentence. If you give your listeners a few seconds to catch up with you, they'll probably fill it in for you.

4. Here is a chance to encourage audience interaction: "Who can tell *me* (pause) some names of *animals* (pause) *with* (pause) horns? Yes, a cow, very good. Yes, a rhinoceros, a yak, a giraffe, a wildebeest, an elephant (elephants have tusks, we'll let them on), an antelope, a gazelle...very good. A buffalo, a bison, a unicorn, a moose."

The pauses suggested here play an important role in audience participation. By building them in, I'm slowing my speech—and question—down a bit so that my listeners can catch up with me. If you rush headlong through the question you may be met by an unsettling silence while the audience processes it. By slowing down as you invite the audience's feedback, their response "flows in" with your narrative.

There is also a tendency in school performances for the youngest kids to sit in the front and the oldest kids in the back. This sort of moment allows you to engage the older kids, especially if you direct your eye contact toward them. These kids will come up with a number of responses and "model" for the younger ones.

5. Just before I call to the captain for the last time, I tell the audience, "And I need your help." Invariably, they join in for the last attempt—the one that successfully reaches the captain's ears!

6. Allow yourself to pause before you complete the sentence here. It will engage your listeners' curiosity so that they fully appreciate the humor of the line.

Little Frog and Centipede

A Folktale from the Haya People of Tanzania

RETOLD BY SUSAN KLEIN

Recommended audience: Junior-high and high-school grades.

In the mid-1980s, I sat on a bench perched on a bluff overlooking a lake in New Hampshire as the (now) Reverend Doctor Charles Rwakatare told me "Little Frog and Centipede." I was enchanted with this tiny cautionary tale told traditionally by Charles's people, the Haya tribe in Tanzania, who tell stories to guide and warn their children and to teach moral and ethical values. He graciously gave me permission to adapt and tell the story in performance and to record the adaptation on my cassette, *Willie the Bug-Man,* and to publish it here to share with all of you. Since then I've told it at workshops and festivals, at schools and special interest group performances and it has become a signature story. It's an uncomplicated yet efficient story, doing its work in a short time with only a few words and images.

SUSAN KLEIN currently resides on Martha's Vineyard in Massachusetts where she was born and reared. She has been featured at more than sixty-five storytelling festivals nationwide, including the National Storytelling Festival. She is author of *Through a Ruby Window: A Martha's Vineyard Childhood,* has produced eight recordings, and directs storytelling audios for other tellers. She is a much sought-after performer, workshop leader, and storytelling coach.

BILL MINIER

LITTLE FROG AND CENTIPEDE

Once there was a frog and there was a centipede.

Little Frog said to Centipede, "Oooh, I love the way you shine! Where did you get that shiny skin?"

Centipede said, "Well, my Little Frog, I will tell you. Once, I told my mother to take a pot, and in that pot to put some oil and make that oil to boil..."

"And then you jumped in!" shouted Little Frog.

Centipede looked at him strangely and said, "No, I did not say that, Little Frog. I will start again...Now, once I told my mother to take a pot, and in that pot to put some oil and make that oil to boil..."

"And then you jumped in!" interrupted Little Frog again.

"No, I did not *say* that, Little Frog! Who is telling this story, anyway? I will start again. Once I told my mother to take a pot and in that pot to put some oil and make that oil to boil..."

"And then you jumped in!" Little Frog shouted, jumping up and down.

"Little Frog, you are making this a very long, long story. Now, I will start *again!"* Centipede was very irritated. She took a deep breath and began again, "Once, I told my mother to take a pot, and in that pot to put some oil and make that oil to boil..."

"And then you jumped in!" shouted the little frog leaping high into the air.

"All right, Little Frog, you seem to think you know my story even better than I know it myself. So you go ahead and tell this story to anyone you want to, in any way you want to. I do not care! I am going home. Goodbye!" And Centipede went home on all her dozens of legs.

Little Frog headed home, too. When he got there, he said, "Oh, Mama, Mama, Mama! I want you to do something for me very bad, very bad, very bad!"

"What is it Little Frog?"

"Please, take a pot, and in that pot, put some oil and make that oil to boil!"

Well, that Mama Frog loved her Little Frog very much, and she would do anything for him. So she took a pot, and in that pot, she put some oil and she made that oil to boil.

And I bet you can guess what that silly Little Frog did!

Yes, he did! He jumped into that boiling oil and he became burned and scarred and ugly. And even to this day, frogs are still so ugly!

So now each time you look upon a frog, you become a witness to the results of Little Frog's impatience.

A WORD FROM THE WISE

This story only takes three and a half minutes to tell so it's perfect to toss in between longer selections. Despite its brevity and its animal characters, I like to do this one with older students. First, I ask them if they ever find themselves in charge of mischievous younger ones (usually I get a fifty to seventy-five percent response based on hands raised).

I proceed with a brief description of the ways people worldwide educate their children—heavy disciplines, cajoling, rescinding privileges, complete freedom—then I say something like "Here's how my friend, Charles Rwakatare, showed me his people in Tanzania teach their children to behave..." and launch into the tale.

At the end, I mention that any time the students find themselves governing disruptive little ones, a story just might do the trick. I suggest they assign whatever annoying behavior the child is exhibiting to an animal, and have the animal repeat that behavior numerous times in the story until something untoward happens. Then, just like Charles's grandfather would have said to him, you can say, "You don't want to become a little frog (monkey, rabbit, etc.), do you?" I tell them this can be a painless and even joyous way to raise children—a whole lot more effective than bopping them over the head, which is a useless way to teach anyone anything.

Dog Tails

A Folktale from the Iroquois People of North America

DOVIE THOMASON

Recommended audience: Grades 3–6.

It's difficult to find Indian people who don't have a version of this story in their culture; it is so widely told and enjoyed. I first heard it from Iroquois (Seneca and Oneida) friends up in New York and Canada, though I've since tracked various versions of it from coast to coast. Other races and cultures have similar stories, I've been told, with varying degrees of "scatalogical reference," if you get my meaning. This version is a nicely "cleaned up" version, appropriate for just about any age and any setting, though it's best audience is schoolchildren from third to sixth grade.

DOVIE THOMASON has been recognized nationally and internationally for her ability to share a glimpse into Native American cultures through the traditional stories she first heard from her Plains Apache grandmother in Texas. For much of her adult life, she has traveled to schools, libraries, festivals, and powwows, sharing the stories that were—and still are—so lovingly shared with her by tellers and elders of Native American nations across the continent. Her workshops on telling cultural stories are often performed at universities and are a stimulating part of conferences and festivals.

DOG TAILS

Many people do not know how dogs came to live in our houses. Many people never wonder why, of all the animals, it was the dog who came to sleep near the fires of human beings. I have been told by many Indian people, of different nations (or tribes) all across what is now called America, that it was the women who decided to make a friend of the dogs.

Long ago, so long ago no one can remember the time, there were no dogs—only wolves. But the women watched the wolves and saw how they were family animals, just like human beings. They cared for each other's young, stayed together for life, and did many things like two-legged people did. The women decided to take a puppy of the wolves and raise him gently, with human beings. And so they did, for generations and generations, breeding tame puppies with others until, after countless generations, there were dogs.

The dogs were given special privileges not given the other four-legged animals. The humans fed them, allowed them to sleep by the fire in the longhouses, gave them names, and played with them. In return, the dogs were great helpers to human beings, as they are to this day. They helped with the hunting, they dragged heavy loads, they carried burdens on their backs, and guarded and protected the home and children.

Since it was decided the dogs were to live with the human beings, the women devised one rule. "You must never think you are a human being, just because you live with us," they told the dogs. "We are two-legged people and you are four-legged people. That is how we are each meant to be, as decided by the One Who Made Us. You are not to do as we do, but to be dogs."

The dogs said nothing, but you could tell that they understood what had been said to them and they never acted like human beings.

Truthfully, they never *wanted* to. When the dogs met together and spoke about the rules (for they *do* speak together, even to this day), they made it clear what they thought of the strange ways of the two-leggeds:

"They are so clumsy! Two-legs are not so well-balanced as four-legs!" laughed one of the dogs.

"And they can hear nothing until it is almost upon them! And no sense of smell that is worth anything!" joined in another dog.

"Their young are slow to grow and cannot help themselves for a long while… It seems they are weaker than our people," another dog thought out loud.

"But they can dance," said a small dog, so softly he could barely be heard.

"What? *What?* What did you say?" asked all the dogs.

"They dance and sing and we can't," said the small dog, almost afraid to say his thought out loud.

"Don't say that! Don't think about that! Don't even get an idea about trying anything like that! The Rule! Don't you dare forget The Rule!" All of the dogs growled and snarled at him at once and then scattered to go back to the comfort of their warm longhouses and meals. They were afraid to even think about what the small dog had said.

But that thought, once planted in their minds, grew and grew until it seemed it was the only thing they could think about at all. So one day all of the dogs snuck away from their homes and human families and met in a clearing, deep in the forest.

"We are far away from our longhouses and human beings, so I am not afraid to speak," said a large dog. "We know they cannot hear us." Many of the dogs laughed at that—low, deep laughter. "I think we should talk about dancing and singing because I don't believe there is anything the humans can do that we cannot! That is why they made The Rule, so we wouldn't learn the truth!"

"It would do no harm," said another dog. "Not if we just tried it once to see what it was like. No one would ever know and we would never speak of it again. It would be our secret!"

Though there was discussion, there was not much. For each dog had been dreaming of dancing, his feet moving in his sleep by the fires of many longhouses, and they were ready to try. One of the dogs ran quickly back to the village and stole away with a burning stick clenched in his jaws.

When the others saw him running back with a piece of the forbidden human fire, they stacked sticks in a great pile. Soon a bonfire was blazing. They looked at each other, wondering who would be bold enough to break The Great Rule.

"I'll do it!" shouted a dog, pushing with his forepaws against a tree until he stood upright on his hind legs. He took two staggering, stumbling steps before falling to the ground.

"I'll help!" cried out another. And together, the two dogs pushed and climbed on each other until they were both balanced on their hind legs. "Look at us!" they yapped. "We're dancing!" The two dogs stepped from side to side in a hopping step. One of them threw back his head and howled, "Yyeeooowww! I'm singing!"

Soon, all of the dogs were on their hind legs, hopping from side to side in a great circle, yipping and howling. They circled the fire, dancing and singing, "Look at us! We are human beings! We dance! We sing!" And they laughed and howled all the harder.

Suddenly, one of the dogs dropped to all four paws and shook his head at the others. "You should see yourselves. We look stupid. Human beings have no tails dragging on the earth as they dance... we just look foolish!"

"Then take off your tails!" cried out a dog, who missed not a step of his dance as he reached behind himself and snapped his tail off and threw it on the ground. In a heartbeat, all of the dogs snapped off their tails and threw them on the great furry pile. Then they began to dance with such singing and howling that it woke the human people in the village.

The dogs were having such fun, dancing and singing, that they never heard the people approaching through the trees until a woman's voice cried out, *"Dogs! What are you doing?"*

The dogs instantly dropped to all four legs, ready to run for home before the humans could see clearly which of them had broken The Rule. They were in such a mad rush... "Wait!" shouted a dog.

"Our tails!"

So great was their haste, and so afraid were they of the angry humans, that each dog dove into the great furry pile, grabbing the first tail he could and sticking it on before running for home. They were in such a hurry that not a single dog grabbed the correct tail.

And that is why, to this day, when a dog meets another dog, the first thing they do is sniff each other's tails, looking for the ones they lost so long ago.

A WORD FROM THE WISE

The best advise I can give is: Have fun with this! Work on some dog voices (you're going to need several), have a good howl, and stagger around a bit like you just discovered the joys of walking on two feet! The sequence of the story is simple and easy to keep straight; so, depending on your listener's reaction, you can exaggerate and stretch the "drama" unfolding as the dogs begin to sing and dance.

I think women tellers can have particular fun with this one, as there's little argument that women domesticated the dog to get a strong, working animal to share their load. And it was *her* load; remember that the Iroquois were (and are) a matrifocal culture, with all property "belonging" to the women. That knowledge can add a twinkle to the she-teller's eye!

SERVED WITH A TWIST

The Farmer's Fun-Loving Daughter

A Folktale from the British Isles

TAFFY THOMAS

Recommended audience: Middle school grades.

I am very conscious that I am a part of a British oral tradition, a link in the chain, and as such, I urge those who hear my stories to pass them on. Much of my repertoire of some three hundred or so tales has never been committed to print; even stories like this one that have been printed I wish to see lifted back into a verbal form to be passed between friends as soon as possible. I hope the readers of this book will go to it.

After training as a Literature/Drama Teacher at Dudley College of Education, TAFFY THOMAS taught for several years in Wolverhampton. He founded and directed two popular theater companies, Magic Lantern and Charivari, until a stroke at the age of thirty-six sidelined him. After his stroke, Taffy turned back to storytelling as a self-imposed speech therapy. He has a repertoire of more than three hundred stories, tales, and elaborate lies, collected mainly from traditional oral sources, which he is happy to tell in almost any situation. His work as a storyteller-in-residence for South Lakeland District Council in 1995, plus many shorter residences, has provided a unique opportunity to further add to this repertoire and his experiences as a performer. He is now one of the leading storytellers in the north of England, if not Great Britain.

THE FARMER'S FUN-LOVING DAUGHTER

There was once a farmer who lived in an enormous house with 161 rooms. He had two sons and a daughter. The sons were intelligent, hard-working chaps, but the daughter was a fun-loving partygoer. The farmer was in the autumn of his years. The time was fast approaching when he would die, and he needed to make provisions for his house and land. He made a will that said the day he was buried each of his children would receive one pound. With this pound they each had to buy something to fill every room in the house from ceiling to floor. If they could succeed in this task they would inherit the farm. Safe in the knowledge that he'd made his will, the farmer took to his bed, and three days later he died peacefully.

The following day the three children took his coffin to the churchyard and they laid him in the ground full of years. They then went back to the farm for cold ham sandwiches. (Now you won't necessarily know this, but you always get cold ham sandwiches at an English funeral. In fact, Maude Coulthard, a traditional storyteller in the Durham dales, always refers to a funeral as "a slow walk and a ham sandwich"!) After the cold ham sandwiches, the family sat down for the reading of the will. The lawyer said, "Your father has willed thus: you each get one pound"—the three children groaned—"and with that one pound you have to buy something to fill every room in the house from ceiling to floor. If you can accomplish this, you will inherit the farm."

The eldest son tackled up his horse and cart and set off around the country buying every secondhand feather mattress and lugging them home to the farm. He dragged the mattresses into the house, slit them open with his knife and filled every room from ceiling to floor with...*feathers*. He told the lawyer he'd done it but the lawyer replied that he had to check every room. It took him so long to walk around 161 rooms that by the time he came to the last one the feathers had settled and there was a gap between the top of the feathers and the ceiling. So he had failed.

The second son set out with his pound and returned sometime later with a small cardboard box full of candles. He set a candle up in every room and lit them. He then announced that he had filled every room from ceiling to floor with...*light*. Once again the lawyer set out to check every room. It took so long that by the time he reached the last room the candle had burned down and the room was in darkness. So he too had failed.

That left the fun-loving partygoing daughter. She set out with her pound and returned with a pennywhistle. [penny whistle, jaw harp, or harmonica depending on what or who is available to assist the storyteller]. She opened every door in the house and sat down crossed-legged in the hall playing a lively tune [at this point in the tale a jig or a reel played live will enhance the performance]. The mourners were still circulating around the house. Hearing the music, some of them started to smile, some to tap their feet, and some to even dance.

At the end of the tune the lawyer said, "Very good, but so what?" The daughter replied that she had filled the house not once, not twice, but three times. She said, "Firstly, I filled every room from ceiling to floor with... *music*. Secondly, people started to smile so I filled every room with... *joy*. And if you put music and joy together then you have... *life*. So even at the time of my own father's death, I filled every room in his house with life." Everyone was so impressed they decided she should inherit the farm.

Now whether she gave up going to parties and became a good farmer or whether she carried on having fun I don't know. You'd have to ask her that, because she is the farmer's fun-loving daughter.

A WORD FROM THE WISE

Whenever possible I like to collaborate with folk musicians. This story is best shared in performance between a storyteller and the player of a pocket folk instrument, say a pennywhistle, a jaw harp, or a harmonica. A few years ago, I was staying in a youth hostel in Saffron Walden, Essex, England. Over a late-night mug of tea the hostel wardens asked me if I'd ever heard the story of the farmer's fun-loving daughter. I said I hadn't. Further mugs of tea were called for, and my repertoire was expanded. On hearing the tale recently, Dan Keding similarly used it to extend his repertoire, albeit with a different title.

The Piper's Revenge

A Folktale from the Scots-Irish Tradition

BILLY TEARE

Recommended audience: The story is suitable for listeners from age 10 to adult.

I have heard at least five different versions of "The Piper's Revenge," which comes from the Scots-Irish tradition. In some versions, the action takes place in Scotland; in others the piper travels to Ireland and specifically to county Antrim. I heard one version from Nancy De Vries (a dear friend and Michigan storyteller who will be much missed in the storytelling world) that had been given to her by the legendary traveler-storyteller, Duncan Williamson. The version I tell I heard originally from Amy Douglas. It is a story that can be told in many settings. It is quite wonderful because it is a ghost story that is not a ghost story that eventually becomes a ghost story. There is also quite a lot of humor in it, which increases as the audience gradually realizes what is happening. Then, of course, there is a brilliant twist at the end.

BILLY TEARE comes from County Antrim, Northern Ireland, and spent many years as an actor, stand-up comedian, and memory man before he began telling stories in 1990. He is now one of the foremost storytellers in Ireland and is much in demand working in schools, hospitals, and day centres at home and abroad. He has performed extensively in continental Europe and throughout the English-speaking world. He has appeared at many festivals in the United States, including the National Storytelling Festival.

THE PIPER'S REVENGE

Once upon a time, and a merry old time it was too, a piper had come from Scotland to Ireland to play his bagpipes for anyone who cared to listen. This was in the summertime and he played for people making hay in the fields, in small villages, and on farms. He would be fed and given a few coins and sometimes he would be put up for the night. Occasionally he would have to sleep out in the open, but this was all right for him in the summer and in the autumn too.

In the winter there were fewer and fewer opportunities for him to play his pipes, and fewer and fewer people gave him a bed for the night. And so his plaid became more and more raggedy, and he looked more and more bedraggled.

So it was that one cold winter's night he was trudging along the road. Now it was a freezing cold night, and the snow was being blown into drifts. He had been to a particular farm asking for a night's lodging but the farmer had said, "Go on, clear off. I don't want the likes of you around here!" And so he walked away.

As he walked through the snow his feet were freezing because his boots were letting in. The soles had let go of the uppers. Just then he tripped over something lying on the ground. He couldn't see what this was because it was all covered with snow.

It was a moonlit night, and as he brushed the snow from around this lump he discovered that it was a brand new boot. Just a wee bit away from this, there was another lump in the snow, and he brushed the snow away from that and it was another brand new boot. So he said to himself, "Great! A pair of brand new boots! And nobody seems to own them, so I'll have them." But he wasn't able to get the boots out of the snow because, you see, there was a pair of feet inside the boots, and when he brushed more snow away he saw a pair of legs, and a body, and arms, and a head. This was the corpse of a poor old man who had collapsed and died in the snow, and he was frozen solid.

The piper looked around and there wasn't a house in sight—nothing but snow-covered fields and ditches and trees, so he thought, *Nobody seems to have missed this auld boy anyway. I'll have his boots.* And he tried to get his boots off, but he couldn't because the boots were frozen solid to the dead man's feet.

Now the piper not only played bagpipes, but he made and repaired them as well so he reached into his kitbag and found a wee saw. *This auld boy doesn't need his boots and come to think of it, he doesn't need his feet either,* he thought. So he picked up one leg and sawed the foot off. Then he picked up the other leg and sawed that foot off. Then he put the feet with the boots on them into his kitbag and slung it over his back.

He trudged back along the road till he came to the house where he'd been turned away a while before. When he knocked on the door, the farmer came out and said, "I told you to clear off once before tonight, and if I have to tell you again, I'll set the dogs on you!"

The piper was just about to walk away when the farmer's wife came to the door and said, "Look, I'm sorry for my husband's behavior. He's just a cross, grumpy old man. You know what they're like. But I'll tell you what—you see that shed across the yard, that's where we keep the cows in winter. We have twelve cows there and the heat of their bodies keeps the air warm in the shed, even on a cold night like tonight. So if you go in there, you'll find some hay and straw, and you can make a wee bed for yourself."

The piper thanked her very much. Just as he was about to walk across the yard she called after him, "Oh, by the way, piper, don't settle down to sleep anywhere near the black cow at the end of the row. She's a wee bit snappy and she might bite at you."

So he walked into the shed, found some hay and straw, and made a wee bed. Before he settled down to sleep for the night, he got the dead man's feet and boots out of the kitbag, took them over to a cow that had lain down, and shoved them in underneath her body so that the heat of her would thaw out the feet and the boots.

He woke up about four o'clock in the morning and took the boots and feet out from underneath the cow. They were well thawed out by now. He pulled the boot off one foot and then the other, set the feet down, and put the boots on his own feet. Then he walked about saying, "Ah, these are a grand pair of boots, they'll do me fine."

And then a thought occurred to him: he didn't much like the way the farmer had treated him and he remembered what the farmer's wife had said about the black cow at the end of the row being snappy, so he took the dead man's feet and put them into his old boots, and then he took the boots and the feet over to the black cow and left them down right in front of her at her head. Then he walked off around the back of the shed to where there was a wee window that he could look through.

It wasn't too long before the farmer's wife came in to milk the cows. She looked all around for the piper, but couldn't see him anywhere. She saw the boots and feet lying over by the black cow and she said, "Oh, heavens! The cow has ate the piper! Husband, quick, come here! The cow's ate the piper! Look! All that's left of him is his boots and feet! What are we going to do?"

When the husband saw this, he said, "Oh, we're going to be in serious bother if anyone sees this, because after all we own that cow. What'll we do at all?"

His wife said, "Well, nobody really knew that piper too well, so all we can do is take the boots and feet out round the back of the shed and bury them, and nobody'll think one thing about it, they'll just think he went back to Scotland."

So the farmer and his wife picked up the feet and took them round the back of the shed, where they brushed some snow away and dug a wee hole. They buried the feet and boots in it, covered it up with soil, and covered the soil with snow. This had been such a shock to them that they went back into the house and poured a couple of mugs of tea with plenty of sugar in them, and a wee drop of whiskey.

They were just about to take a sip of the tea when they heard the skirl of pipes coming from outside. The wife went over and looked out of the window, and there, standing on the ground where the boots and feet had been buried, was the piper playing his bagpipes. The farmer ran over to the door, opened it, and looked towards the piper. "Oh no!" he cried. "It's the ghost of the piper come back to haunt us!"

Now, as the farmer and his wife were looking out at him, the piper started to look back at them and advance toward them across the yard, playing his bagpipes all the while. They were that terrified, they took to their heels and ran off down the lane, with the piper hot on their heels playing his pipes as he chased them. They had such a fright that they ran off like a couple of sprinters.

Soon the piper let them run on. He stopped and said to himself: "Ho ho, it'll be a while before they come back."

He returned to the house where the door was lying open. He went inside, and there on the stove was a big pot of tea and beside a frying pan a plate piled high with bacon and sausage. As the piper hadn't seen food for a good few days he licked his lips. Near the stove was a crock with eggs in it so he lifted an egg, cracked it into the pan and fried it. Then he ladled some of the bacon and sausage onto a plate along the egg, poured himself a big mug of tea, and sat down at the table to enjoy it.

He was just about to eat the first mouthful when he heard three loud knocks at the door. He rose and went over to open the door. There stood a poor old man, chittering and shaking with the cold. The piper said to him, "Och, ye poor aul man ye, come on in and have some food and drink. Sit up to the fire to warm your poor feet…"

The old man stared blankly back at him and said in a rasping voice, "I would warm me feet—if I had any to warm!"

A WORD FROM THE WISE

When telling to school audiences, you may want to drop the reference to "whiskey" when the couple have a drink of tea to calm their nerves. Otherwise, this is a favorite for middle grade audiences.

I find no need to go into great detail about the removal of the old man's feet. I normally imitate the sound of a saw for just a few seconds. Whenever the wife enters the cow shed and can't find the piper, I become quiet as she looks around for him, mimicking her head movements. Then when she sees the feet and boots, I scream. So the combination of first silence and then screaming makes the audience both jump and laugh at the same time.

The Sky is Falling

An Urban Adaptation of a Cautionary Tale

JAY STAILEY

Recommended audience: Urban school audiences.

When I began gathering stories for a collection on the culture of poverty, I would never have believed Chicken Little would become a player. But she appeared from Miss Wilson's back yard, and when that delivery truck hit a pothole shaking loose a piece of mortar from the old brick building nearby, the chick seemed a perfect destination for the mortar.

This simple folktale is wonderful for those who have heard the classic version and want to play with what happens when the sky falls in a city setting; urban kids hearing it for the first time may connect to Chicken Little in these more familiar surroundings.

Ultimately this story cautions us that we have enough challenges without creating more where none exist. The lesson here is that seeing only small but alarming pieces of the big picture can make us prisoners of our fear.

JAY STAILEY is a parent, principal, professor, author, storyteller, and adventurer. A two-time winner of the Greater Houston Area Liars Contest, Jay teaches a class on Storytelling in Education at the University of Houston at Clear Lake. He is a former chairperson of the National Storytelling Association and the 1999 winner of the International Reading Association's Presidential Award for Reading and Technology. Jay also launched the www.islandstories.com

digital storytelling site where he has published *Short Tales, Tall Tales and Tales of Medium Stature,* stories about his island neighborhood. In July of 1998, he released a collection of traditional stories entitled *Think Rather of Zebra: Dealing with Aspects of Poverty through Story.*

THE SKY IS FALLING

One day a little chick slipped through the fence and out onto the sidewalk. A delivery truck roared by on its way to the Main Street grocery. The noise of the truck alone might have frightened that little bird to death, but when it hit a pothole the whole street shook. When the whole street shook, a little piece of mortar rattled loose from the bricks in the building and came down with a *thump* right on top of that little chick's head.

"Oh my gosh," the chick said. "The sky is falling!" She raced off to tell the other birds. "The sky is falling! The sky is falling!" she cried as she ran along the fence.

Miss Wilson's big hen came fluttering out of her tin roost. "What's that? What's that?" she clucked. "The sky is falling?" She looked up at the blue beyond.

"Yes," said the chick. "A piece of it fell and hit me right here on the head."

The hen saw a bump on the chick's head and assumed the worst. She flew up over the fence and joined the chick's cry of alarm.

"The sky is falling!" they shouted as they bustled through the vacant lot.

A warty Muscovy duck had waddled up from the city park. He was so fat from the crumbs of the park visitors he had long since forgotten anything he once knew about flight and the sky. "The sky is falling?" he asked with alarm in his voice.

"Yes! A piece of it hit this little chick in the head."

"We better tell the others!" the duck said, leading the parade of alarmists toward the park.

"The sky is falling! The sky is falling!" the threesome shouted as they waddled into the park.

"What's that?" the formerly wild goose said, looking up from her search for bugs amidst the park litter. "I knew this would happen someday. That's one more entitlement down the drain." The goose joined the wild chase.

Coyote—the last of the country folk to move to the city—was lurking in the woods by the park. As the fearful feathered foursome passed close by he heard the hen cry, "We must find a safe haven or we will all die!"

"Haven or heaven," the others chimed in. "The sky is falling! The sky is falling!"

With that, the sly coyote stepped out and said, "I know just the place. Quick, follow me!" and he headed through the woods toward the highway.

Those foolish birds were so excited they never thought to compare catastrophes. They followed coyote into the woods and out by the highway, where coyote pointed to a dark round culvert. "The sky can't fall on you in there," he shouted, looking skyward with mock alarm. He moved aside to let the plump fowl step into the darkness. Then, licking his chops, he turned to follow.

At that very moment, the same grocery truck that had loosened the mortar that sent the birds scurrying, swerved on the highway to avoid yet another pothole. A crate of potatoes became airborne and landed with a *thud* on the hungry coyote. The little chick, watching from the dark culvert, looked up fearfully toward that circle of blue sky. Turning toward the other birds she said, "Move further back. It's worse than I thought!"

A WORD FROM THE WISE

Any story with talking animals gives the teller lots of leeway with voices and movement. Give each new character a unique voice and physical traits, or invite audience participation by having different listeners take on the parts. If the birds in this tale are unfamiliar, you can always substitute a more familiar species.

In this tale of classic alarmists, one can stir the feathered friends into quite a frenzy by speeding up the rate, tone, and movement as the perceived catastrophe is heightened with the addition of each new panicked voice. The teller can bring on his best Mr. Smooth when the slick coyote finally arrives at the scene, though it's best not to make him too likable or the listeners may be distracted by his demise and miss the little chick's final miscalculation.

The Edge of the World

A Folktale from the British Isles

RICHARD WALKER

Recommended audience: Middle school grades.

Rowena Walker writes: Mostly Richard told stories about places he knew, but obviously this story doesn't fit into that category. He used it to caution against blaming personal setbacks on "bad luck," and as a counterpoint when he heard someone, students in particular, make the comment, "It's not fair." As this story goes, in some circumstances, we create our own luck.

RICHARD "MOGSY" WALKER, from Cressage in Shropshire, took the first steps toward being a storyteller about 1975, when he was the leader of a portable theater company, "Cat's Whiskers," which did a good deal of its work within the folk scene. As Richard said, "Most members of the company had their own solo piece to offer, and as I could neither play an instrument nor sing in tune, I started performing monologues and then moved into storytelling." From those beginnings he became one of Britain's leading storytellers, appearing in venues throughout the U.K., including the Edinburgh Festival. He was the first English storyteller to appear at the National Storytelling Festival. He has written two books, *The Barefoot Book of Trickster Tales* and *My Very First Book of Pirates*. Richard died February 15, 1999. He will be greatly missed by story lovers everywhere.

THE EDGE OF THE WORLD

There was a young man who lived on a mountaintop in a beautiful redwood house. Though he had everything one could want, he still had this nagging feeling that something was missing from his life. Actually, he was bored. *I have no luck,* he thought. *I wonder why.*

He thought and thought and thought but could not figure out why he had no luck. Finally, he asked a wise woman and she told him, "Only God can tell you that."

"Where do I find God?" he asked.

"At the edge of the world," she answered.

So he set out walking toward the east to find the edge of the world. He walked for a day, a week, a month, a year, a year-and-a-day until he came to a clearing. There were wolves on either side. On the left were a group of beautiful furry wolves mingling and glowering at him. He went to the right, and there was a skinny, scrawny wolf sitting and staring at him.

"Where are you going?" asked the scrawny wolf.

"I am going to the edge of the world to ask God why I haven't any luck," he answered.

The wolf said, "Can you do me a favor and ask God why I am not strong and powerful like my brothers and sisters?"

"OK," said the young man, and he set out walking toward the edge of the world. He walked a day, a week, a month, a year, a year-and-a-day until he came to a small skinny tree standing among the taller trees reaching up to the sky with their many branches and leaves. One of the leaves fell off and floated to the ground as the young man approached.

"Where are you going?" asked the small tree.

"I am going to the edge of the world to see God and ask him why I don't have any luck," he answered.

"Could you do me a favor?" asked the tree. "Ask God for me why I only have a few branches and have not grown tall like the other trees in the forest."

"Sure," said the young man and set out walking. He walked a day, a week, a month, a year, a year-and-a-day until he came to a lovely house surrounded by a picket fence. He opened the gate and found a garden with colorful flowers creating a splash of beauty around a neat white house. He knocked on the door and a beautiful woman opened the door and greeted him with a smile.

"Oh, how wonderful for you to stop by. Do come in." The woman cooked him a wonderfully delicious dinner, and they ate and talked until late into the night. Finally, she asked, "Where are you going?"

"I am going to the edge of the world to find God and ask him what happened to my luck," he answered.

"Oh, when you see God, can you ask him for me why I am so lonely?"

"Sure," he said.

He rested that night and the next morning set out walking. He walked a day, a week, a month, a year, a year-and-a-day until he came to the edge of the world. He looked out and sure enough, on a blue-white cloud, there stood God.

"God," he called out. "Why don't I have any luck?"

God folded his arms and looked hard into his eyes. "Because you are stupid," he roared. "I have given you luck. It is all around you before your very eyes, but you never see it."

"What do I do?" he asked.

"Keep your eyes open. Luck is all around you."

The young man started to ask God the other questions, but God interrupted him saying, "I know what you are going to ask. I'm God and I know everything!" God floated over to him and whispered the answers in his ear.

The young man set off to find his luck. He walked for a day, a week, a month, a year, a year-and-a-day until he came back to the woman's house. Again, he knocked on the door, and again she invited him in and cooked him a wonderful supper.

"This is the best meal I ever ate," he told her.

"Thank you, but tell me—did you see God? What did he say?"

"God said that if you find a husband, you will not be lonely."

"Wonderful," said the woman. "Will you be my husband?"

"I'm sorry," said the young man, "but I have to find my luck. I don't have time. But I'll send back the first nice man I meet to be your husband."

He walked a day, a week, a month, a year, a year-and-a-day until he came back to the scrawny, skinny, shaky tree. "Did you ask God why I'm so scrawny?"

"It's because there is a treasure chest buried right under you and it is blocking your roots from getting nutrition."

"Marvelous," said the tree. "Over there are some shovels that some working men left. Please get the shovel and dig down and remove the treasure chest."

"Oh, I'm sorry, but I don't have time now. I have to find my luck. But I'll tell you what I'll do. I'll send the first strong man I meet to help you."

He set out walking again. He walked a day, a week, a month, a year, a year-and-a-day until he came to the scrawny wolf.

The excited wolf asked, "Did you ask God why I am so scrawny?"

"Yes. It's because you are not eating enough. You are not getting enough nutrition. God said that you should eat the first stupid animal you see."

And that is exactly what the wolf did.

A WORD FROM THE WISE

Richard told this tale in a very straightforward manner. He didn't give great emphasis to voices or gestures. He didn't get in the way of the story. This is the kind of tale that will work no matter how you tell it.

It is easy for the listener to identify with the man in the tale who is never satisfied. We have all been that man. The story is deeper than the simple plot line suggests. Keep the telling direct and uncomplicated. Voices for the various characters could enliven it and add your personal touch...but essentially, keep it simple and let this age-old tale work for you.

This story would be appropriate for a wide range of listeners 10 years old to adult.

—DH

The Praying Mantis

An Original Story

DEBORAH JOY COREY

Recommended audience: Grade 5 and up.

Bill Mooney writes: In 1992, following a storytelling session in Princeton, New Jersey, an elderly man handed me a copy of *Yankee* magazine and suggested that I read a story in it called "The Praying Mantis." He said he couldn't get it out of his mind and thought it would be a good tale to be told. Its effect was just as indelible on me. I wrote to Ms. Corey and asked her permission to tell it. She not only graciously agreed but sent along several other wonderful stories as well.

While I tell this story to anyone over ten years old, "The Praying Mantis" is a big favorite in middle schools. It is one of those wonderful stories that "kick in" instantly. The opening line grabs listeners by the throat and doesn't let go until the narrative comes to an end. It is also a story that engenders a lot of discussion once the students are back in their classrooms. I love telling this story and I know you will, too.

DEBORAH JOY COREY's stories have appeared in many magazines and quarterlies. Her novel, *Losing Eddie,* won the SmithBooks/Books in Canada First Novel Award. Ms. Corey developed the book as a stereodrama for C.B.C. Radio, and it is now being developed for film. She is a native of New Brunswick, Canada, living on the coast of Maine with her husband and two daughters.

SUSAN WHITE

THE PRAYING MANTIS

Laura Lowell is about as ugly as a girl could be. Her daddy says she's got a face worse than dirt and she knows he's right.

Laura works at the Hinky Dink, a little greasy spoon in one side of a gas station. She's the main waitress and mostly works alone because the place is never too busy for one to handle. There are a couple of booths made out of old car seats and a few chrome tables and chairs and a long counter with stools at the very front, which is where most everyone likes to sit.

Despite Laura's ugliness, she can cook, and a lot of men like to come in the evening after an unsatisfying supper at home. Laura notices that most men order meat and that they prefer it a little pink rather than well done. She's been known to serve a few bleeding burgers to those customers who complain too often about dryness.

The Hinky Dink is a gossip pit, and Laura has good ears. She knows just about everything that's been said about everyone. But even more important, Laura remembers all the people who have made remarks about her looks, and she keeps a mental list.

On Sundays and in the early mornings, Laura takes long walks in the yard around her daddy's house. She always carries a small net and a jar with holes punched in the top. She's a bug collector. She's probably got the biggest collection of bugs of anyone who's ever lived. She's partial to beetles and has quite a few. She says ants are too common, but she's still got a load of them, along with other regular things like spiders and houseflies and lightning bugs. Her favorite is the praying mantis, and she has two. One at home under her bed, and one in the kitchen at the Hinky Dink along with a few other bugs she keeps there for company and also for revenge.

When Laura knows for sure that a customer has been mean to her because of her looks, she likes to chop up one or two bugs real fine and serve it up to him in his hamburger or just spread it on top of whatever he's having as if it's black pepper. She considers this the most beautiful way of getting even, because the customers hardly notice anything strange, and if they do, they just leave their food in front of them like they were already sick or something before they came in.

Once, a man Laura considers to be a show-off said right to her when she was taking his order, "Your face would make a great dartboard."

All the men at the counter smirked, and Laura just went back into the kitchen and made his order up. She chopped a lot of spiders real fine. Chopped, chopped, chopped them until they were powder and cooked them in his meat like spices.

She slid the show-off's plate along the counter.

"Here's your order. Hope you enjoy it."

She watched him chomp down his burger. Laura likes to chew bubble gum, and she smacked real good while she watched him. He ate it all and then settled down for a bit. After a while, he got a little pale and while Laura was totaling up his bill, she heard him say to his friends, "I think I'll get on home. Feel like I'm coming down with a bug or something."

Laura threw her head back. "Ha, ha, ha, ha, comin' down with a bug. I ain't ever heard that one."

Every night around eight-thirty, a bachelor named Darrel comes in and sits at one end of the counter. Things are usually pretty slow then, and Laura is always standing with her elbows on the cash register, staring out into the smoky room and blowing bubbles.

Darrel says, "Evening, Laura. What are you up to?"

"Nothin'."

Darrel spreads his legs over one of the counter stools and sits down. He is a small round man with white hair at his temples and his skin is slimy with big pores. He has a glass eye that stays still while the other eye looks around. "Just chewing your cud, are ya, Laura?"

"Cows have cuds, Darrel, I don't."

Laura gets her yellow order pad and slouches in front of Darrel, her face all droopy. "What do you want?"

"Don't be mad, Laura. I didn't mean nothing by it."

"Why don't you just say I'm ugly, Darrel? That's what you mean when you talk about me chewing my cud."

"I don't think you're ugly, Laura. I like the way you look. Why would I come in here every night if I didn't like your looks?"

"My eye, you like my looks."

"I do, Laura. Nothing's worse than eating and looking at something ugly. I wouldn't do it. I'd rather play with a snake first."

"Liar."

"I am not a liar, Laura. I like you."

"What do you *want?* Do you want to eat or do you just want to listen to yourself talk stupid all night?"

"Burger...with cheese and onions." His good eye is floating back and forth out of embarrassment.

Two men come in and sit up at the counter. They order coffee, and Laura splashes it down in from of them, then hustles back to the kitchen.

She gets out her praying mantis to cut up for Darrel's burger. It's a hard thing for her to do because she figures they're not that common, but she does it just the same, and she leaves it in big pieces so that Darrel will be able to taste it. She holds onto its hind legs before cutting it and the lime green body reflects on her fingers. She cuts the head off first. The blood comes out in spots on the cutting board and Laura swallows her bubble gum, like she's gulping her regret. She can hear the two men talking back and forth—talking about some farmer's pigs that failed to pass inspection, and how people can get sick if they spend time with unhealthy pigs.

Laura serves Darrel his burger. He looks at her and says, "Wish you'd believe me."

Laura turns and goes back to the kitchen. She watches Darrel eat his burger. He looks straight ahead at the counterfeit dollar bill that's pasted on the wall, and he chews hard with his mouth closed. His pores get a little damp. He looks like he knows what he's eating, but he keeps on going just to prove something. When he's almost finished, Laura goes out and fills up his coffee cup. She can hear something cracking between his teeth.

"When are you gonna get married?" one of the men teases Laura.

"Never."

Both men laugh. They throw some quarters on the counter for their coffee.

The other one says, "Why don't you marry Darrel here?"

"Darrel's too old. I told you I ain't getting married, never."

The men leave the restaurant, and Darrel slides the money for his burger out to the edge of the counter and leaves it there. Laura looks at the money. "Don't tip me."

She goes back into the kitchen and fills up ketchup bottles until Darrel leaves.

She watches the narrow part of his back until he's outside. She wrings out her dish rag and takes it out to the counter. She throws the two empty coffee cups into the dirty dish pan and reaches for Darrel's plate. There is a hard round thing the size of a tiny ball mixed in with the crumbs and Laura leans over to see what it is. One side is clear. She lifts up the plate and it moves around in a circle. She looks closer as it rolls toward the edge of the plate, and right beside her blood-stained thumb, she sees Darrel's glass eye.

A WORD FROM THE WISE

Give each of the characters in the story a particular voice; this helps eliminate the "he said, she said" problem. It also helps to "become" Laura and Darrel, smacking your gum as you say Laura's lines, for instance. Just be careful not to overact and get in the way of the story. I urge you to adhere as closely as you can to Ms. Corey's exact wording. The story simply does not work as well when it is paraphrased.—*Bill Mooney*

The Tail of the Linani Beast

A Folktale from Western Kenya

MARGARET READ MACDONALD

Recommended audience: This remarkable story thrills all ages. For small children, it is a lively participation story; for older youth, a serious story to think about. It particularly needs to be heard by the latter.

Kenyan folklorist Ezekiel Alembi, to whom I am indebted for information about this story, tells me that the linani appear in many tales. He notes also that the area from which this tale comes is known for its palm trees. This telling is expanded from the briefer telling by John Osogo in *The Bride Who Wanted a Special Present and Other Tales from Western Kenya* (Kampala: East African Literature Bureau, 1966). My telling is shaped also by watching The Whitman Story Sampler's lively version.

MARGARET READ MACDONALD, a children's librarian in Seattle, earned a Ph.D. in Folklore from Indiana University. She has offered her "Playing with Story" workshops in Kota Kinabalu, Songhkla, Whakatane, and Mahasarakham. MacDonald's work includes *Traditional Storytelling Today: An International Sourcebook* (essays from world folklore scholars); *Earth Care: World Folktales to Talk About;* and *Shake-It-Up Tales: Stories to Sing, Dance, Drum, and Act Out*. MacDonald and her performing partner, Richard Scholtz, have just released their second audio recording, *Cockroach Party,* a lively companion to their previous cassette, *Tuck-Me-In Tales.*

THE TAIL OF THE LINANI BEAST

There was a young man who fell madly in love with a beautiful girl.
Every day he would go to her house and beg her to marry him.
She wouldn't say yes and she wouldn't say no.
She would say something like...
"You know... I am really thirsty for some coconut water.
It would be really nice to have some coconut water right now."

The young man would jump up.
"You want coconut water?
I'll *get* you coconut water!"

He would run to the coconut grove,
climb a tree, cut a coconut, bring it back,
slice off the top, and give it to her.
"Here! A coconut!"

The next day he would be back again.
"Would you marry me? Please?"

She wouldn't say yes and she wouldn't say no.
"Well... I am really hungry for some fresh fish.
Some fresh fish for supper would be really good."

"You want fish?
I'll *get* you fish!"

That young man would race to the stream.
He would spear some fish.
He would rush back and lay them before her.
"Here! Fresh fish!"

Anything that girl could think of to ask...
that young man would provide.
Still she would not agree to marry him.

One day he asked her...
"Isn't there *anything* I could bring
that would persuade you to marry me?
I would bring you *anything*... *anything* at all."

She got a faraway look in her eye.
"Well there is *one* thing—
but I'm sure you could never bring it—
the tail of a Linani Beast.
I've heard they are so beautiful, so silky, so rare.
How famous I would be if I owned such a tail."

The young man gulped.
"The Linani Beasts live deep in the forest.
The Linani Beasts crunch up humans for their dinner."

"I know.
Any man who brought me the tail of a Linani Beast
would be so *brave*
I would *have* to marry him."

The young man was *inspired.*

Now he knew how to win this girl.
All he had to do was get the tail of a Linani Beast...
and she would be *his!*

He would go at once!
That young man *sharpened* his knife.
He set off into the forest, in search of the Linani Beasts.

The Linani Beasts lived in a grove deep in the forest.
All day long they slept.
But at dusk, the Linani Beasts woke up.
Then they went looking for bones to crunch.
Preferably *human* bones.

The Linani had learned that humans coveted their tails.
So to keep the humans from sneaking up on them
the Linani had developed a strange sleeping habit.
While the Linani slept,
they would keep opening and closing their eyes.
They would *really* be asleep all the while,
even when their eyes were open.

And while they slept they would mutter under their breaths.
When they closed their eyes they would mutter "I'm asleep."
When they opened their eyes they would mutter "I'm awake!"

"I'm asleep… I'm awake!
I'm asleep… I'm awake!
I'm asleep… I'm awake!"

But really they were sleeping soundly all the time.

When the young man reached the grove of the Linani Beasts,
he saw them lying in mounds all over the ground.
They seemed at first glance to be asleep.
But when he ventured closer he saw
they were opening their eyes every few minutes and muttering.

"I'm asleep… I'm awake!
I'm asleep… I'm awake!
I'm asleep… I'm awake!"

"They only sleep for a few seconds at a time.
How will I sneak in and cut off a Linani tail?"

He sat down to observe them.
He watched for a long while.
He noticed that when the Linani opened their eyes,
they never looked around.
He noticed that when the Linani said, "I'm awake!"…
they kept right on breathing deeply as if in sleep.

"I believe the Linani are really sleeping all the time.
I don't think they wake up when they open their eyes."

He had to have that tail.
So he took the risk.
Slowly the young man tiptoed up to the sleeping Linani.
He stepped over the first Linani.

"I'm asleep... I'm awake!
I'm asleep... I'm awake!
I'm asleep... I'm awake!"

The Linani didn't move.

"They *are!* They are all sound asleep!"

The boy tiptoed through the sleeping Linani,
looking for the most beautiful tail.
There he saw it—
the tail of the Chief of the Linani.
Long... silky... *that* was the tail for his girlfriend.
The young man pulled out his knife.
That knife was so sharp... so sharp...
with one quick *slash* he cut the tail right off.

It was so quick,
and the Linani was sleeping do deeply,
that it did not even wake up.

"I'm asleep... I'm awake!
I'm asleep... I'm awake!
I'm asleep... OUCH... I'm awake!
I'm asleep... I'm awake!"

The young man tiptoed out of the pile of sleeping beasts.
He began to *run* back through the forest with the tail.

"Now she will *marry* me!
Tonight she will be *mine!*"
But he had a long way to travel yet to reach his village.

Night began to fall.

Back at the grove the Linani began to wake up.
"Awwnn! Wake up, Linani!
Wake up!
Time to go out and crunch some *bones!*"

The Linani began to stretch and get up.
The Linani beast laying next to the chief sat up.
He put his hand on the ground and felt something wet and sticky.
It was blood from the chief's tail . . . but . . .
"What's this . . . ?"
He began to laugh.
"The chief has wet his bed!
The chief has wet his bed!"

The chief sat up and scowled.
"What?"
The chief put his hand down on the ground.
"What? . . . It's *blood!*
My tail!
Someone has cut off my *tail!*
Only a human would do a thing like this.
Whoever that man is . . . today he becomes my ENEMY!"

The Linani began to snuffle around the grove.
Soon they discovered a trail of blood leading into the forest.

"I go to fetch my tail
and our supper," said the chief.
He picked a handful of straw grass and tied it in a magic knot.

Holding this knot in front of him he chanted,
"You who became my enemy today,
you who became my enemy today,
no matter where you go,
no matter where you hide,
I will find you... SPEAK TO ME!"

And the magic knot of grass drew that young man's voice.
Running down the forest path,
the young man felt himself suddenly answering.
"I...I...I..."
His voice burst out. He could not stop it!
"I who became your enemy today,
I who became your enemy today,
I cut your tail."

The magic knot made him say that.
Then the young man began to call out,
"I didn't mean to do it.
I didn't mean to do it
The woman... the *woman*...
The WOMAN made me do it."

The Linani stomped down the path after that young man.
The young man ran and ran.
Every little while the Linani would stop and call again.

"You who became my enemy today,
you who became my enemy today,
no matter where you go,
no matter where you hide,
I will find you... SPEAK TO ME!"

And the young man would be forced to stop and call back.
"I who became your enemy today,
I who became your enemy today,
I cut your tail.

Oh...but...
I didn't want to do it.
I didn't want to do it
The woman...the *woman*...
The WOMAN made me do it."

The young man reached his village.
He ran to that girl's house.
"Here! Here is your Linani tail!
Now will you marry me?"

She was impressed.
"The tail of a Linani!
How *brave* you must be!
Of *course* I'll marry you."

"Then hide me!
The Linani is coming."

She covered him with mats.
He could not be seen.

The Linani entered the village.
He looked around at all of the houses.
"He is hiding in one of these," the Linani said.
"He who became my enemy today,
he who became my enemy today,
no matter where you go,
no matter where you hide,
I will find you...SPEAK TO ME!"

Under the mats, the young man felt his voice coming out of him.
"I who became your enemy today,
I who became your enemy today,
I cut your tail.
Oh...no...
I didn't mean to do it.

I didn't *want* to do it
The woman . . . the *woman* . . .
The WOMAN made me do it."

The Linani followed the sound of that voice.
He pushed into that house.
There sat the girl, holding his tail.
He didn't see the young man anywhere.

"You who became my enemy today,
you who became my enemy today,
no matter where you go,
no matter where you hide,
I will find you . . . SPEAK TO ME."

Under the mats the young man held both hands over his mouth.
But it was no use. His voice came out.
"I who became your enemy today,
I who became your enemy today,
I cut your tail!"
Oh . . . but . . .

He leapt to his feet and begged the Linani.
"I didn't want to do it,
I didn't want to do it!
The woman . . . the *woman* . . .
The WOMAN made me do it!"

The Linani stared at that girl.
"The woman?
The *woman?*
The WOMAN made you do it?"
He snatched his tail back from the girl.
He turned to that young man.
"But the man . . . the *man* . . .
The MAN is in charge of his own actions."

He snatched that young man up.
He threw him over his back.
He marched out of the house,
    out of the village,
        and into the forest.
That young man was never seen again.

Now in that village they tell the young girls,
    "If you love a young man...
    do not ask of him impossible things.
    Do not *do* that."

And to the young men they say,
    "If you love a young woman,
    No matter what she says,
    No matter what she asks,
    remember that the MAN is responsible for his own actions."

A WORD FROM THE WISE

For strongest effect with older audiences, it is probably best to tell this story without participation. However, when telling to very young children I sometimes ask them to chant, "I'm asleep... I'm awake..." while I tiptoe around among them looking for a good tail to steal.

My daughter Jen and her husband, Nat Whitman (The Whitman Story Sampler), perform this in a lively tandem piece with one prop... the tail. Nat stares balefully into the audience as the Linani chief and terrorizes them with his "I'm asleep... I'm awake..."

The Dancing Fiddle

A Folktale from Scotland

DAN KEDING

Recommended audience: Age 10 to adult.

I travel to Great Britain and Ireland often to perform at festivals but it was my very first visit that yielded this story. I learned it in 1981 in Scotland on a bus trip from Stirling to Dunblane from the great fiddle player Tom Anderson. As we rolled through the Scottish countryside, he told this story in low, conspiratorial tones, and at the end he slowly nodded and swore that it was true. I've been telling it ever since that meeting. If you and I ever meet on a bus or a plane or a train, I'll tell you this tale and I'll swear it's true and for us, it will be.

DAN KEDING is a storyteller and ballad singer. Since the early seventies he has traveled internationally weaving traditional tales, ballads and folk songs, original stories, and personal narratives into his performances. He has been featured at the National Storytelling Festival and at festivals throughout the United States and Great Britain. His recording "Rudy and the Roller Skate" won the 1999 American Library Association Notable Recording Award. He lives in Urbana, Illinois, with his wife, Tandy, and his Australian Shepherd, Jack.

RON ACKERMAN

THE DANCING FIDDLE

Once, in the north country of Scotland, there lived a pawnbroker. Now this man had a reputation for being honest and fair—and this reputation earned him the respect of all the people in town and in the countryside. One day, a woman came into his shop carrying a fiddle case. She put it down on the counter and said, "I'd like to sell this old fiddle."

"Let's have a look, shall we?" The pawnbroker opened the case and saw a fiddle of golden spruce and flamed maple, with a carved lion at the top of the peg head.

"I have to admit, 'tis a fine looking fiddle," he said. "But beauty doesn't always make for a grand instrument. If I give you too much, and it's not worth it, I'll be cheating myself—and if I give you too little, and it's worth a lot, I'll be cheating you. Let me keep the fiddle overnight, and tomorrow I'll stop by to see my friend Tom Anderson and ask him what he thinks. He knows all there is to know about fiddles. Come back about noon and I'll tell you what he said." The woman agreed and left the fiddle.

The pawnbroker carried the fiddle home with the intention of visiting Tom the next morning. Since he didn't own the fiddle, he decided to put it in his bedroom to keep it out of harm's way. He stood the case on its end in a dark corner of the room.

That evening friends came to visit the pawnbroker and his wife for dinner, and after their meal they enjoyed cards and conversation and a bit of whiskey to keep away the chill of the night. After the guests left, the pawnbroker went to bed. He fell asleep at once—but, in the middle of the night, he awoke as an unearthly music filled the room. At the side of the bed, the fiddle case lay on the floor, open and empty. To his amazement, the fiddle suddenly came into view, spinning on its end pin in a macabre dance—the strings vibrating as it twirled faster and faster.

The pawnbroker rose, reaching for the instrument. In an instant, he was grabbed by the throat. He struggled in vain against invisible hands that were slowly choking the very life from him. His wife awoke to see the indentations of unseen fingers that pressed deep into his flesh. She screamed—throwing herself forward—and as she lurched out of bed, she knocked the fiddle to the floor. At that moment, as the fiddle lay still and quiet, the murderous hands released their prey.

Gasping, the pawnbroker staggered to an open window. He filled his lungs with the cool night air. In the street below, a tall man stepped from the shadows and stood in the light of the street lamp. A jagged scar ran down the man's forehead, through his brow, and down his cheek. A chill went through the pawnbroker as their eyes met. He was staring into the face of evil itself. The man sneered at the pawnbroker and walked away into the night.

The next morning the pawnbroker didn't bother to stop at Tom Anderson's house. He went straight to his shop and put the fiddle in the farthest corner. At noon, the woman appeared. He slowly pushed the fiddle across the counter.

"I want nothing to do with this instrument," he said.

"Isn't it a good violin?" said the woman.

"Good?" exclaimed the pawnbroker. "It almost killed me last night." He told her the story of the dancing fiddle—and the strange music—and the invisible hands that choked him. As he showed her the purple bruises on his neck, he watched her face grow ashen. "And," the pawnbroker continued, "I don't know who your friend was, but..."

"Friend? What friend?" She spoke in a voice barely above a whisper.

"The man beneath my window, with the long scar down his face."

Slowly, the woman reached for the fiddle and backed away from the pawnbroker. She clutched it against her body.

"That was no friend," she whispered, "that was my husband." For a moment, she hesitated. "We were poor—I often needed money—but he swore that if I ever sold this fiddle he'd kill the man who ever bought it." She put her hand on the latch and slowly lifted it. "He died ten years ago."

The woman walked into the street—and the pawnbroker never saw her again.

A WORD FROM THE WISE

This is a story that doesn't need a lot of dramatics from the teller. A conversational tone will bring your listeners into the realm of the story's truth, and therein lies the strength of the story—making the audience believe its true. A soft voice—almost as though you are letting the listener in on a secret—will make this story scarier than a lot of shouting and jumping. Use measured tones, letting the ghostly mood of the story take over for the listener.

Remember, Tom Anderson swore to me it was true.

CODES OF CONDUCT

The Story of Anniko

A Folktale from Senegal

CHARLOTTE BLAKE ALSTON

Recommended audience: All ages.

This is my adaptation of *Anniko!* by Molly Melching (Les Nouvelles Edition Africaines, 1978). The story was given to me by Molly as a gift during my second visit to the country of Senegal in 1989. The songs were sung into my tape recorder by our guide, Bollé Mbáye, who was also a musician and storyteller.

The story was originally told in Wolof, the dominant indigenous language of the Senegambia region. Molly's original version is written in French and begins, "It was very far, this small village. So far that one could not find the way back in a day. This is where Anniko found herself..." I created the village scenario in the beginning and tell this version with the permission and blessing of the author. The remainder is very close to the written text.

As with many traditional Wolof stories, *Anniko!* was created to reflect on several important, shared cultural values held by the Senegalese. This story makes an impact everywhere I tell it. The message is both timeless and timely, given America's increasingly diverse population—and the negative response some have to that diversity.

©PATENTED PHOTOS

CHARLOTTE BLAKE ALSTON tells at schools, universities, museums, and festivals throughout North America, including the National Storytelling Festival and the National Festival of Black

Storytelling. She is the recipient of numerous awards, including the 1997 Commonwealth of Pennsylvania Artist of the Year Award (the Hazlett Memorial Award). She is a featured performer on the Carnegie Hall Concert Series and hosts the "Cargenie Kids" preschool concerts. In addition, she hosts "Sounds All Around," The Philadelphia Orchestra's preschool series, and often serves as host and narrator on family and youth concerts. She was selected as one of five Americans to present at the first International Storytelling Conference in Accra, Ghana, in the summer of 1999. She resides in Lansdowne, Pennsylvania.

THE STORY OF ANNIKO

There was once a little girl named Anniko who lived very happily in a village with her mother, father, sisters, and brothers until—one day—a very sad thing began to happen. A sickness came to her village and swept through like an angry fire. No one was spared—except Anniko.

Anniko was grief-stricken and lonely, but she knew she could not remain there. Sadly, she began walking away from her village. She walked and walked until she found herself standing at the edge of a thick, thick forest. There were stories of this forest—stories of those who had entered it but had never returned. There were also stories of a village on the other side of that forest where, just as in Anniko's own home, a stranger would be welcomed in. But she would have to enter that thick forest in order to find the path that would lead her to that village.

Anniko uttered a silent prayer before she entered that thick forest. She walked and walked, pushing aside wide leaves and long vines. She grew tired, but she continued on. Well, her prayers were answered that day, and she came to the path that would lead her to the village. She followed that path to the other side of the forest.

What a beautiful country this is, Anniko thought as she walked. Soon the village came into sight and the villagers all came out to greet her. It was then that Anniko noticed that these villagers had one rather unique characteristic. They all had long necks with heads that sat at the tops of their necks. Even their babies had long necks with little heads at the top. Anniko had never seen anything like this before.

The villagers were about to greet Anniko, but they couldn't believe their eyes. She had a short neck—much like yours and mine. They had never seen anything like this before and they weren't quite sure what to do or say. One of them asked what a little girl like Anniko would be doing in that forest alone. Anniko began to tell all that had happened to her, her family and her village. Something about Anniko made the Longnecks trust her, so they invited her to stay.

They were right. Anniko was warm, caring and respectful. She worked, danced and played with the villagers. She accompanied the Longnecks to the marketplace and shared in their celebrations and their sorrows. But the thing that was most special about Anniko was that every morning, very early, Anniko would rise and cross the village singing:

Yee si naa leen
Yee si naa leen yen
Yewu nama deyman
Te yee si naa leen itam
Yewu jotnaa
Yee si naa leen
Yee si naa leen yen

which means: *I'm coming to wake you up. I'm up, a new day has begun. I'm coming to wake you also, people.*

Singing was very much a part of Anniko's life in her old village but, unbelievable as it might sound, the Longnecks had never heard singing before. They thought this was a wonderful way to be awakened each morning. Soon they would not get up and go about their work until they heard Anniko's sweet song. They loved her even more because of this special gift she brought to them.

But in this village—as in all villages in the world—there was one evil, jealous, small-hearted man. He had not liked Anniko from the first day he saw her because she was different. One day he called to her and said, "You do not belong here. You are different from us. You have a—short neck! Differences can only lead to problems in this village. You should take yourself away to avoid bringing trouble here!"

The words stung Anniko's heart. Without thinking, she ran off and found herself in the middle of that same thick forest. The rainy season had come so the vines hung longer, the leaves had grown larger, the foliage was thicker…

and Anniko became afraid. She could not even see where she was stepping so after a while she stopped and rested. Night fell quickly.

Early the next morning, all the Longnecks lay in their beds waiting to hear Anniko's sweet song. But there was only silence. One by one, they began to rise from their beds and ask, "Where is Anniko? Have you seen Anniko?" They gathered in the center of the village, and one of the elders said, "I think I know who might know something. Follow me." He led them to the home of that evil, jealous, small-hearted man who told them—almost with pride—how he had spared the village of problems by sending away the different one.

The villagers were furious. They had to think of a way to help Anniko find her way back. They could not go into the forest because they would become lost themselves. One of Anniko's friends had an idea. She said, "Maybe we can sing as Anniko has sung to us. Maybe she will hear our voices and that will help her find her way back."

Well not only had the Longnecks never heard singing before Anniko's arrival, they had never tried to sing themselves. They agreed it was important to try. They decided they would sing Anniko's name and tell her they were sad and wanted her back. So they all stood side by side in the center of the village and began to sing for the very first time:

Anniko ni sa wa ni
Anniko ni sa wa ni
Anniko ni sa wa ni
Wo, wo, wo chi ka nay, nay, nay
Wo, wo, wo chi ka nay, nay, nay
Hey, ho bi ci ni
Hey, ho bi ci ni

which means: *Anniko return quickly. Wo, wo wo, we are sad without you. He, ho, we ask you to return.*

They sang and sang, stronger and stronger. Their voices traveled quickly into the forest and reached the place where Anniko sat. When she heard the singing, she knew it was the Longnecks trying to help her find her way home. She followed the sound of the voices to the path that took her into the village once again. The villagers rejoiced when they saw that she was safe with them. They invited her to stay with them as long as she wished.

The chief of the village said to Anniko, to the villagers, and to that evil, jealous, small-hearted man: "It is not the length of your neck that is important. It is the goodness of your heart."

A WORD FROM THE WISE

In telling this story, I try to convey with my voice and facial expressions a sense of foreboding (without being overly dramatic) when describing the forest. I deepen my voice as I describe and speak as the "evil, jealous, small-hearted man." Anniko's "singing voice" is light and not one with the vibrato of a mature adult or trained voice.

As the villagers begin to sing, I falter, crack my voice, sing hoarsely, hesitate, cough, and fidget through the first four lines and gradually get stronger. After "finding their voices" on the last two lines, I often invite children's audiences to participate by saying, "Well, it was a good start, but there was something missing. It is the voices of everyone who has ever lost anyone or anything close to them. So you can help the Longnecks sing stronger by using your hands and your voices to chant Anniko's name." I lead them by chanting and clapping in a slow 4/4 pattern: *"Anniko! Anniko! Anniko! Anniko!"* The children continue chanting as I sing the song stronger and faster.

I sing the songs as Bollé taught them to me. You may choose to create your own melody and/or not use the Wolof words at all.

PRONUNCIATION GUIDE

Anniko's Song

Yay see näh len
Yay see näh len yen
Yeh woo näh mäh day mähn
Tay yay see näh len ee-tähm
Yeh-woo jote näh
Yay see näh len
Yay see näh len yen

Villagers' Song

Anniko nee säh wäh nee
Anniko nee säh wäh nee
Wo wo wo chee ka näi näi näi
Wo wo wo chee ka näi näi näi
Hey ho bee see nee
Hey ho bee see nee

Deer and Jaguar Share a House

A Folktale from Brazil

ANTONIO ROCHA

Recommended audience: Grades K–8.

I first heard this old tale when I was a child back in Brazil; my mother, who is in her seventies now, also heard it as a child. Many years later I performed it around the United States with The Light Theatre Company in a show about the rainforest.

What I love about this story is the innocence of the characters and the profound message about the importance of communication. With all the technological advancements we have today, the world is getting smaller and smaller. The cultures of the world have to learn how to live in harmony and respect differences; we have to communicate with each other in order to solve conflicts. Unfortunately, in this tale our "dear" characters don't.

This is an old tale with a clear and present truth. Tell it and enjoy.

ANTONIO ROCHA, a native of Brazil, began his career in the performing arts in 1985. Three years later he received a Partners of the Americas grant to come to the United States to perform and deepen his mime skills with master Tony Montanaro. Since then he has studied with master Marcel Marceau, earned a Summa Cum Laude Theater BA from the University of Southern Maine and toured nationally with the Light Theatre Company. Mr. Rocha has performed his solo shows of mime and tales from the Far East to the Far West in such venues as the Singapore Festival of the Arts, Aruba International Dance Festival, the New England Modern Storytelling Festival,

RHONDA FARNHAM

Three Apples Storytelling Festival, Washington Storytellers Theatre First International Festival at the Austrian Embassy, the Kennedy Center Imagination Celebration, and educational institutions around Maine and New England. Mr. Rocha is a member of the Maine Arts Commission, LANES, The New England Foundation for the Arts, and the National Storytelling Association.

DEER AND JAGUAR SHARE A HOUSE

One day Deer was wandering along a riverbank. "I am tired of wandering here and there," he said to himself. "I would like to build a house." He looked around. "And where could I find a better spot to build a house than here? This is where I will build."

So Deer went back into the woods, making plans to return.

Now, on that same day, Jaguar was also wandering along the same riverbank. "I am tired of hunting here and hunting there," he said. "I would like to find a place to build a house and settle down." He looked around with surprise. "And where could I find a better place to build a house then here? This is where I will build."

So Jaguar left, making plans to return.

The next day Deer returned and started working on his house. With his great antlers he cleared the ground of all its bushes and shrubs. Soon he grew an appetite and returned to the forest.

While he was gone, Jaguar also returned. When he noticed that the ground had already been cleared he roared with confusion. He looked left, then right, then looked up with a smile of understanding. "The God Tupan must be helping me build my house. What great fortune!"

So Jaguar built the floor of the house, then left for his evening kill, making plans to return.

The next day Deer returned and almost tripped on the floor. "The floor is already built. But...who...when...?" He looked left, then right, then looked up with a smile. "Ah, the God Tupan is helping me build my house. What great fortune!"

So Deer built the walls of the house and left, making plans to return.

The next day Jaguar returned. "What a great job," he said to himself as he admired the walls. He put on the roof of the house and left, making plans to return.

The next day Deer returned. "Tupan, it is beautiful!" he exclaimed. The deer then built two rooms in the house—one for himself and another in gratitude for Tupan. After he finished his work the deer went to sleep in his room.

That same night Jaguar returned. "Two rooms in the house?" he remarked. Then he heard a sound. "Someone is snoring... It must be Tupan. I will take the other room." And Jaguar lay down for the night.

The next morning both animals woke up at the same time. It was hard to say who was more surprised when they come out of their rooms. Jaguar let out a roar.

Deer stammered, "Did you help me build my house?"

"Did you help me build *my* house?" Jaguar retorted.

"Um, yes," Deer said warily.

"So," said Jaguar, "let's share it."

Share the house with a jaguar? Deer thought to himself. But aloud he said, "OK."

So Deer lived in one room and Jaguar in the other room.

One day Jaguar approached Deer and said, "Please prepare the pots, water, and a nice fire. I am going hunting now."

So Jaguar went deep into the woods. There, he started to stalk his prey.

He followed it, hiding himself in tall grass. At the right moment, he sprang forward and chased after it.

Roarrr! And so he killed another deer.

He took the deer back to his house. When the deer with whom Jaguar was sharing the house saw what supper was all about, he lost his appetite. He entered his room but he could not sleep. He feared that Jaguar would come and eat him also.

As Deer lay awake all night long he came up with a plan. Early in the morning he said to Jaguar, "Get the water, the pots and pans, and a nice fire. I am going hunting now."

"Hunting?" Jaguar said with surprise.

"Yes," said Deer.

So Deer went deep in the woods. There he found a huge jaguar sharpening his claws against the bark of a tall tree. Off to the right he spotted Tamandua Bandeira.

Tamandua Bandeira is a large anteater with a flaggy tail. Legend says that when this animal is aggravated it stands on its hind legs and gives a fatal embrace to its opponent—fatal because its curved and sharp claws pierce his opponent's lungs during the embrace.

Deer approached Tamandua and said, "Tamandua, that jaguar over there has been saying terrible things about you."

"Can't you see that I am eating now?" said Tamundua huskily. "Yum yum yum... I love these ants."

"Tamandua," Deer repeated, "that jaguar over there has been saying terrible things about you, your sisters, your mother... the whole family."

"Did you say my mother? Ahhh, just a second! Let me square something off with this jaguar!" He lumbered back through the woods to the jaguar. "Hey, Jaguar!"

There was no answer. The jaguar continued to sharpen his claws.

"Hey, Jaguar!" he called again, louder this time

The jaguar turned to face Tamandua. Quick as lightning, Tamandua embraced him, and that was the end of that jaguar.

After the deed, Deer picked up the jaguar's carcass and took it home.

When the jaguar with whom Deer was sharing the house saw what supper was all about, he lost his appetite.

That night neither Deer nor Jaguar could sleep. Each feared the other. There was no trust.

As the hours passed, they started to get tired. Deer's eyes began to close. When they did, his head nodded and his great antlers hit the wall with a loud noise. *Bam!* When Jaguar heard the noise, he leapt up into the air, roaring with fear. When the deer heard the roar, he leapt up and ran out of the house along with Jaguar.

They took a quick look at each other. Deer ran east. Jaguar ran west. And since that day, Deer and Jaguar have never lived together.

A WORD FROM THE WISE

Although telling a story is a very personal thing, the teller has to find a way to connect with the audience in order to succeed. When I performed this story with The Light Theatre Company, we employed masks, mime, and shadow play. Since then I have performed it for many years alone, in black, with no masks but lots of movement. I become the animals and at times I even stop the verbal narration to narrate with movement. This comes from my strong background in mime.

I believe that one should always keep this tale light and humorous with just a few serious pauses during the most dramatic moments of it. Please do not gloss over the lies Deer tells to Tamandua; that is part of the lesson the audience members have to hear, whether they are children or adults. It is easy to recognize Jaguar's physical fierceness, but as we say, Deer's words have an equally destructive power. Have fun, enjoy, and please always mention how you got this tale and where it comes from.

Pronunciation: The God Tupan is pronounced "two-pun." Tamandua Bandeira is pronounced "tah-man-doo-AH band-AIR-uh."

Tales of Aesop

Fables from Ancient Greece

HEATHER FOREST

Recommended audience: Age 8 to adult, as well as family audiences.

The plot lines of these ancient tales were created by the storyteller Aesop in Greece twenty-five hundred years ago. Aesop was a black storyteller who lived in ancient Greece. Legend has it that he was originally brought from Africa as a slave. Because of his humble position in society, Aesop could not speak his thoughts openly. Yet he powerfully commented upon human nature and the society around him through his metaphorical fables and stories. Aesop's storytelling earned him his freedom and he rose to great renown and respect in his time.

Since then countless storytellers have preserved the tales by retelling them and passing them on through the oral tradition. The plots attributed to Aesop can be appreciated for their simplicity or considered more deeply for their metaphorical meaning. As a musician, I enjoy the rhythm and sound of language. Sometimes, purely for the pleasure of word play, I weave dialogue or rhyme into my prose renditions.

HEATHER FOREST weaves a musical spell with the magic of words. Her minstrel style of storytelling blends original music, guitar, poetry, prose, and the sung and spoken word. She has created seven storytelling recordings, four children's picture books, and two folktale anthologies. As a performing artist, her vividly crafted language, evocative facial

LUCAS FOGLIA

expression, and graceful gesture create powerful images in the minds of her listeners. She has toured her repertoire of world folktales since the mid-1970s to theaters, major storytelling festivals, and conferences throughout the United States. She is a recipient of the National Storytelling Association's Circle of Excellence Award.

THE GIRL AND HER BUCKET

A young girl was going to market with a bucket of milk on her head. "With the gold that I get from the sale of this milk, I'll buy a red hen," she said to herself. "The hen will lay eggs, they'll hatch, and then I'll have many chicks to raise. I'll feed them well and when they're grown, they will each lay eggs. And those eggs will hatch and I will have more hens, who'll lay more eggs that will hatch into chicks…

"Before long I'll be rich and I'll wear fine clothes with emeralds and rubies from my collar to my toes. And one day perhaps I shall visit the Queen. I will bring her rare gifts from China. I'll enter the court with my arms full of treasure. Bowing low I shall say, 'For your Majesty's pleasure!'"

And she bowed low…

With that sweep of her arm, she knocked off the bucket and spilled her fantasy load.

"Oh dear," she cried. "My dreams are splattered in puddles of milk on the road…"

YOU ARE BEAUTIFUL AS YOU ARE

There was once a crow who did not like his feathers.

"I wish I were a peacock!" he would say.

"You are beautiful as you are!" the other crows insisted.

"How plain and dull you seem to me!" he'd complain, and fly off to admire peacocks.

The peacocks strutted about with their colorful tailfeathers outstretched. To the delight of the crow, some of the peacock feathers lay on the ground when the peacocks left.

Crow flew down to the ground and stuck the feathers into his wings and tail. He attached a few sticking up from his head.

"Now I am as beautiful as a peacock," he said.

But when he went to join them in their strutting, the peacocks poked him and pecked him. What a fuss!

"You are not a peacock," they said. "Don't imitate us!"

Bruised and still dragging some broken peacock feathers in his tail, he returned home.

After all his insults, no one wanted his company!

As he sat alone, the other crows said, "It's foolish to try and be what you're not. Learn to love the feathers you've got!"

EVERYONE AGREES TO PEACE

A sly fox tried to trick a rooster into coming down from his perch.

"Brother Bird," the fox said, "come down and have a friendly chat!"

"No," said the rooster. "I'm sure you'd eat me."

"Oh, I wouldn't," said the crafty fox. "Haven't you heard? Everyone has agreed to live in peace."

"Is that so?" said the rooster, who was just as crafty.

Stretching his neck, the rooster pretended to look at something far off in the distance.

"What are you looking at?" asked the fox curiously.

"Oh... just a pack of hungry fox hounds headed right this way."

Upon hearing this, the fox trembled in his tracks and ran off.

"Come back!" crowed the rooster. "Why are you running away? I thought you said that everyone has agreed to live in peace."

"Well, perhaps those hungry hounds haven't heard about it yet," said the fox, and he bounded away.

QUARRELSOME CHILDREN

There once was a man who had quarrelsome children. Even on his dying day they bickered.

"My last wish," he said, "is for you to bring me a bundle of sticks."

When this was done, he gave each child one and said, "Take your solitary twig in hand and break it."

Crack! Crack! went the dry, old wood as each child broke a solitary twig.

"Now," he said, "bind them together. Tie them, and you'll see how much stronger your brittle twig can be."

The old man passed away.
His children never forgot that day.
Though they each lived separate, distant lives,
Each sister,
Each brother,
In times of trouble they bonded together like a bundle of sticks,
Giving strength to one another.

MICE IN COUNCIL

A terrifying cat had come to live in the big house. Every time the mice went into the kitchen for a nibble, the cat would send them scampering.

"We'll starve!" they shouted, and decided to have a council meeting. One by one the mice spoke, but no one could think of a plan.

Finally, a boastful mouse stepped forward and proclaimed his idea to be best. He explained, in detail, how a small bell attached to the cat's collar would warn them all of his approach. Patting himself on his own back for the excellent idea, he sat down.

The oldest mouse stood up and said, "You are a very clever fellow to think of a plan like that! But now tell us, are you *brave* enough to put the bell on the cat?"

A WORD FROM THE WISE

Tellers who have kept Aesop's fables alive through the centuries usually add a personal touch. Countless contemporary renditions can be found in the 398.2 section of your public library. I invite tellers to take these plots and find an expressive way to present them for modern audiences. Add a touch of music, allow your voice to portray the characters, or turn them into a play. Remember an experience from your own life that is similar to the theme of the fable and weave your own tale into the ancient one. These tales ring "true" not because they actually happened but because there is some "truth" in them. Have you ever daydreamed, like the girl who dropped her pail of milk? Have you ever longed to be different, like the crow that lusted after peacock feathers? Has an elderly person ever taught you an important lesson, like the father of the quarrelsome children? Read over these fables, then drift into your own life story.

The Secret of the Animals

A Folktale from the Huron People of Québec

MICHAEL PARENT AND JULIEN OLIVIER

Recommended audience: Grade 6 through adult.

This story was told by Mme. Prudent Sioui, a *Métis* of the Huron people of Laurette, Québec. Folklorist Marius Barbeau notes that stories of the *Métis*, passed on by the elders, contain ancient elements of kings, kingdoms, and castles that can be traced back to France and to the Native American tradition, where animals talk and leaves possess healing powers.

We often recoil at the violence we find in old stories, as we recoil at the violence in our own world. So, we ask, "What is the point? Why tell this story now? Why was it told in the first place?"

Stith Thompson points out that this is "one of the oldest and best known of folktales in Oriental and Medieval literature"—perhaps because it reminds us that there are certain human bonds that we betray at our peril.

CATHERINE EMORY-BRICKER

After many years in Charlottesville, Virginia, MICHAEL PARENT recently returned to his native Maine. He is a storyteller, writer, workshop leader, singer, and juggler. He has performed at the National Storytelling Festival, the "Open Border" Quebec-United States Cultural Exchange Performance Festival, and the International Festival of Storytelling. Many of the stories in his repertoire reflect his French-Canadian heritage.

JULIEN OLIVIER is a third-generation Franco-American from Manchester, New Hampshire. Storyteller, lecturer, and writer, his work draws from family lore, fieldwork, and oral history research in New England. He has also studied and traveled widely in the French-speaking world and has worked with traditional arts agencies in New England and the Smithsonian Folklife Festival. A former educator, TV producer, and newspaper columnist, he now works as a translator and as a correspondent for CBC/Radio-Canada. Julien and his wife, Jane, have four daughters and make their home in Barrington, New Hampshire.

Parent and Olivier are co-authors of *Of Kings and Fools: Stories of the French Tradition in North America.*

THE SECRET OF THE ANIMALS

Once upon a time there were two orphans. One day the older brother said to the younger, "We are indeed so poor that we will soon die of hunger!"

"What can we do?" the other asked.

"Well, we could earn a living by begging, but you would have to be blind. If you will trust me in this, I will show you how it is done. But first, I must put out your eyes. Then, good people will have pity on us and will give us alms. I guarantee you that we will make money; in fact, we'll make lots of money."

The younger brother, who had always been respectful of his older brother's ideas, answered, "OK, go ahead, but only on one condition: you must never abandon me, or I will die."

So his brother put the young man's eyes out; and off they went from city to city, begging for their sustenance.

At the end of seven years, they had not only survived but had accumulated a handsome sum of money. But the elder brother had by now become quite tired of having to lead his younger brother around. As they walked along a river one day, the older one pushed his brother into the water. The lad was thrown downstream, unable to contend with the current. Soon, the river became shallow; and, as the blind brother thrashed about, his hand struck a branch. He grabbed the tree and pulled himself out onto the shore. He felt night approaching and, not wanting to be prey for the wild animals, located a tree and climbed as high as he could.

At least I will escape this night from the ravishing beasts, he said to himself.

Three animals—a lion, a bear, and a wolf—came along the path and stopped beneath the tree to chat. The lion said, "I have a secret."

The bear chimed in, "I have one, too."

And the wolf added, "Well, so do I!"

The lion had been first to speak; so his friends said, "Tell us your secret, and we will tell you ours."

"Well," the lion said, "as you know, the king of the Kingdom of the Three Afflictions is ill. His sickness appears to be incurable. But I know how to heal him."

With little urging, the lion explained, "Under the king's bed there is an enchanted frog. If someone took it away, the king would be instantly cured."

Now, it was the bear's turn. "I know that the frog in the castle is the fairy who drinks the water and dries the land. If her stomach is slit, all the water will pour out, the rains will fall, the springs will gush, the rivers will flow, and the ocean will breathe causing the tides to surge."

The wolf, not wanting to be outdone, hurried to tell his secret. "The oldest prince has been blinded," he said. "If someone rubbed his eyes with a leaf from this very tree above us, the prince would recover his sight."

The three had no sooner shared their secrets than they departed, each in his own direction, to search the forest for prey. From his perch high above the animals' heads, the blind man had been listening. Now, he lost no time. He plucked a leaf and rubbed his eyes. Lo and behold! His sight was restored.

"Fantastic!" he cried out. "Now if the wolf told the truth, the others must not have lied either." Picking another leaf, he hid it in his jacket.

Early the next morning, he climbed down from the tree and headed for the castle.

"Your prince is blind," he told the guards. "I, too, was once blind. I know the secret of his condition, and I can restore his sight."

"How can you restore his sight," they jeered, "when the wisest of men from throughout the entire earth have been unable to help him?"

"Take me to him. I will apply the seeing leaf!"

So they took the young man to the prince, and he rubbed the eyes where darkness had settled. Suddenly, the prince cried out with joy. He could see! His vision had been restored to that of a normal fifteen-year-old. So pleased was he that the prince showered his benefactor with *écus* and lavished gifts upon him. Then, the prince asked if the healer could, perchance, achieve similar results with his old father, the king, who had suffered for a long time from an unknown illness.

"I could cure him," the stranger responded confidently, "but you must leave me alone with him for a few moments, and you must permit me to open the shutters."

After some hesitation, the prince agreed to leave his father alone with the healer; but as to opening the shutters, well, that was another matter altogether. For many years now, the king would not permit the light of day to enter the castle because he did not want to witness the great affliction of his kingdom caused by the terrible drought.

As soon as the young man entered the room, he reached under the royal bed and grabbed the frog that hid there. The king immediately felt an enormous relief. Drawing the frog to himself, the young man then concealed it under his shirt. The king thought he was cured. Yet, when it came to giving his consent to opening the shutters, the king was adamant. No window in his castle was to be opened. So the young man threw the frog back under the bed, and the king instantly became ill again.

He was now worse than before. The king, in fact, could barely speak. "Good physician," he muttered, "I bend to your wise wishes. Open the window if you must."

The young man threw open the shutters and let in the light of day. Then, grabbing the frog again, he threw it out. From the king's tower it fell one thousand feet to the church steeple, where it was impaled on the weather vane. At once, the rains poured from heaven, the brooks gushed forth from the earth, the rivers overflowed, and the oceans produced their tides.

Without fanfare, the young man soon set out on his way along the path leading to the forest. There, he met his brother who had been attracted to the city by rumors of wonders produced there.

"Well, hello, Brother!" the elder said. Then, astounded that the young man had regained his sight, he asked, "Since when are you no longer blind?"

"Since you broke your promise and abandoned me, you miserable brother!"

The cruel one threw himself at his brother's feet. He also noticed that his brother's pockets seemed particularly full. Tearfully, he begged forgiveness as he coveted the jingling *écus*.

"Where do all these riches come from?" he asked, still kneeling.

"They come from the tree of secrets," the young man responded.

As soon as he learned where this tree of secrets was located, the older brother set out through the forest to climb it himself.

When twilight came, the lion, the bear, and the wolf returned along their usual path. They were in a grumbling mood. Someone, some nosy busybody, must have discovered their secrets. They were in a very bad temper. Stopping at the foot of the tree where they first made their revelations, they noticed the man who waited there.

"Vengeance!" they cried. "It is he who betrayed us. He took the leaf and murdered our friend the frog. Devour him!"

And so they did.

A WORD FROM THE WISE

Since the story hinges on the secrets the younger brother learns form the animals, it's important to slow the pace or otherwise underline that part of the story. Since it's a fairly dramatic moment anyway, slowing down the telling will likely enhance the story.

Some tellers may want to give the animals, as well as various human characters, distinctive voices or characteristics. Remember that there are many ways to clarify characters and thus better communicate the story. Here are just a few:

Changing pitch (e.g., Bear—lower voice), pace (Lion—speaks more slowly), attitude (Wolf—speaks with great dignity), posture or distinctive gesture (Older Brother—speaks with arms folded OR often points finger when he speaks; Younger Brother throws arms open). By extension, in dialogue between two characters (e.g., the brothers) Older speaks looking down at Younger and vice versa.

But keep it simple. If you go too far with this character-indicating business, you can end up doing exactly what you were trying to avoid—confusing your audience.

WHEEL OF FORTUNE

Pine Trees for Sale!

A Folktale from Japan

MILBRE BURCH

Recommended audience: I tell this story in settings as diverse as kindergartens to senior centers, though upper elementary school children particularly like it.

The mother of two daughters, I am always on the lookout for stories with active female characters. This gentle story is the Japanese cousin of a favorite Welsh folktale of mine, "Morgan and the Pot o' Brains." My version of that one is found in *Best-Loved Stories Told at the National Storytelling Festival* (National Storytelling Press, 1991). In both stories, a simple, hardworking man is assisted by his fond and clever wife.

Growing up, I was passionate about fairy tales even before I could read. But as a brown-haired, scruffy, adventuresome little girl, I longed for role models who were neither blonde nor sleepy. This is one of those stories that offered the perfect antidote for what ailed me. May it be strong medicine for another generation of young woman.

An internationally known performer, award-winning recording artist, poet, writer, and teaching artist, MILBRE BURCH is a storyteller in every sense of the word. She co-directed the Storytelling Project of the Cotsen Children's Library, and has toured or taught for five state arts councils, the Lincoln Center Institute, the National Conversations Project of the National Endowment for the Humanities, Young

BETH THIELEN

Audiences, the LA Music Center, and the Performing Tree. She has released ten recordings on the Kind Crone label and lives in North Carolina with her journalist husband and two daughters.

PINE TREES FOR SALE!

Gombei was a good man. Gombei was a poor man. Gombei was a man of few words.

Every morning he sat at his table weaving straw into shoes, and these he sold at the marketplace. Every evening he sat on the bench outside his house and wove straw into rain capes, and these he sold at the marketplace. In the middle of the day he plowed and cultivated his rice field so that he would have food to eat and some to sell at the marketplace. He was content, except that sometimes he was lonely.

One evening as he sat down to his meager meal, there was a knock at the door. When he answered it, he saw a young woman standing in the doorway. To Gombei's eyes, she was the most beautiful woman in the world.

She said, "I am lost and alone. I'm tired and hungry. Can you help me?"

Gombei was a man of few words, but he said, "Yes."

And he gave her his meal and he gave her his bed, and he sat up all the night watching over her. And when she awakened in the morning and saw how carefully he had guarded her, she said, "Gombei, I am alone and you are alone. Let us marry and make our lives together."

Now Gombei was a man of few words, but he said, "Yes."

And so they married, and Gombei was so in love with his wife that he could barely take his eyes off of her. In the morning, they would sit together at the table as he wove shoes until his wife would say, "Gombei, stop! No one has feet that big!"

Or they would sit together in the evening as he wove rain capes, until she cried, "Gombei, look! No one is that tall!"

He could hardly bring himself to leave her at midday to go to the field to plow. And no sooner had he reached the far end of the field, then he would drop the plow and run back to the house for another glimpse of her.

Finally she said, "Gombei, we are going to starve. Listen, we have saved a few coins. Take these to the village and pay for my portrait to be painted on paper. Then, we can hang the portrait at the far end of the field, and when you plow down that way, you can always see me. When you turn back to the house, I can wave at you from the window."

It was a good plan. A portrait was soon painted of Gombei's wife. And in it, she smiled out at him with such love and joy that truly she was the most beautiful woman in the world. The paper portrait was hung in the trees at the far end of the field, so that Gombei could plow away from the house and see the face of his wife. Or he could plow toward the house, and there she was waving at the window.

All was well until one day a breeze blew up, and it became a wind and the wind became a gust and the gust lifted the portrait off the tree and blew it, blew it, blew it away. And Gombei was heartbroken. But his wife said, "Gombei, don't worry. We have saved some more coins. We can have another portrait painted."

But perhaps they should have worried. For the wind blew the portrait until it blew over the wall and into the garden of the house of the lord of the province. When his servants brought him the picture, he said to them, "If there is a portrait this beautiful, there is a woman this beautiful. Go and get her for me."

Now his servants had good hearts, but what could they do? They traveled from village to village with the portrait until at last they came to a place where the people said, "Believe it or not, that's Gombei's wife."

And so the servants came to the door of Gombei's house, and when it was opened to them, there stood the woman in the portrait. With heavy hearts, they explained why they had come, and it was clear that if she did not go with them, something terrible would happen to Gombei.

At last she said, "I will go with you. But first, give me a few minutes alone with my husband." The servants had good hearts, and they went outside the house to wait. Then Gombei's wife turned to him and said, "My husband, do not grieve. In a few weeks time the new year will be upon us. On the day of the celebration, come before the house of the lord of the province, dressed in the rags of a peddler with small pine tree saplings upon your back—the kind people buy to decorate their gate posts for good luck and long life. Announce yourself by calling 'Pine trees for sale!' and I will do all the rest."

Gombei was a man of few words, but he said, "Yes." Then they embraced and parted. The servants led the woman to the house of the lord of the province; they showed her through the massive gate and into his garden.

When the lord of the province looked upon her, he said, "You are beautiful. But I see that you do not smile on me the way you smile in this portrait." He was a proud man and so he said, "I will not marry you until I have made you smile."

As the weeks passed, he brought jugglers and jesters, poets and painters, actors, musicians and magicians into his home, but she did not smile upon him. He offered her delicious foods and fine drink; he gave her beautiful clothes and hair ornaments. But still she did not smile. Until new year's day.

That morning Gombei did as his wife had suggested. He dressed himself in the rags of a peddler, gathered many small pine tree saplings, and appeared outside the gate of the lord of the province. There he said all he knew to say: "Pine trees for sale! Pine trees for sale!"

At the sound of Gombei's voice, the woman of the house began to smile softly. "Oh," said the lord of the province, "that is good! But I want better!" And he motioned for her to join him standing at the window looking down upon the peddler outside the heavy garden gate.

Gombei walked back and forth outside the garden saying all he knew to say: "Pine trees for sale! Pine trees for sale!"

The sight of the ragged man with the pine trees made the woman smile all the more. "Oh," said the lord of the province, "I like that! But I want better!" And he bade his servants go down and push open the massive gate and invite the pine tree peddler inside.

In a moment, Gombei found himself in the living room of the lord of the province, and all he knew to say was "Pine trees for sale! Pine trees for sale!" And seeing him so close, his wife went forward and touched the trees upon his back and began to chuckle softly.

"Oh," said the magistrate, "good, good, but I want even better." Turning to Gombei, he said, "Take off your clothes!"

Gombei did as he was instructed, and then the lord of the province gave him his own fine robe to wear so that the nakedness of the peddler would not embarrass the woman. Next the lord put on the peddler's rags and lifted the pine trees to his shoulder. He began to strut about his living room calling, "Pine trees for sale! Pine trees for sale!" And the woman smiled upon him and then pointed eagerly out the window to the street below.

"Ah!" said the lord of the province, "Now I know how to really make you laugh!" and with that he hurried down to the yard and instructed his servants to push the heavy gate open and let him out into the street and then to push the gate closed again after him.

This they did, and the lord began to pace back and forth outside his own house calling, "Pine trees for sale! Pine trees for sale!"

And from the window in his house, the lord heard the lovely, lilting laughter of the woman he had wished to marry. Looking up, he saw her standing in the window, next to Gombei, who was dressed as the lord of the province. And that's when the lord realized that he was standing outside his gate, dressed in the rags of a peddler.

He began to pound upon the door and shout, "Let me in! Let me in!" But his servants had good hearts. And they never opened that gate to him again.

What became of the lord of the province I cannot say. But I can tell you this: Gombei and his wife lived in luxury and love till the end of their days.

NOTE: I first came across this Japanese folktale as "The Wife's Portrait" in Keigo Seki's collection, *Folktales of Japan* (University of Chicago Press, 1963). Since then I have found Seki's version reprinted in Joanna Cole's *Best-Loved Folk-Tales of the World* (New York: Doubleday, 1982) and in a slightly different translation as "The Picture Wife" in *Folk Tales from Asia for Children Everywhere, Book Two* (New York: Weatherhill/Heibonsha, 1976). In the original text, the story is cited as tale type 465, of which thirty-nine versions are mentioned. I guess this makes forty.

A WORD FROM THE WISE

It's not just the words that make a well-told story. It's the pictures in the head of the teller that travel body-to-body to the listener. In working on this or any other folktale, don't concentrate on telling the words alone. Part of your homework as a storyteller is spending time with the story: visiting the place where it is set, or if that's not possible, looking at images of the country, the costumes, the culture of origin so you can really see the landscape and the people in your mind's eye. Use your five senses as you move through the sequence of the tale. It may not change the language you use in telling the story, but it will inform the words you use. And once your homework's done, concentrate on telling the story, not the words—because there will come a day when you are thoroughly distracted in mid-sentence and the words may leave you. If that happens, just look into your mind at the pictures you've made of the story, and describe to the listeners what you see. That way everyone will live happily ever after.

The Bottle Imp

from the story by Robert Louis Stevenson

ADAPTED BY BILL MOONEY

Recommended audience: Grade 4 through adult.

Several years ago, a middle-school principal mentioned to me that she would like her students to hear a series of stories about "choices." She felt it was particularly important for middle-schoolers to hear stories like these since they were reaching a critical juncture in their lives where the choices they made would seriously affect their future. I thought it was a great idea and began looking around for stories that would fill the bill.

While searching for a new and different story for Halloween, I stumbled across Stevenson's wonderful tale "The Bottle Imp." It wasn't the Halloween story I was looking for, but it was perfect for the Choices program. Except for one thing: Stevenson's language is rich and wonderful when it is greeted by the eye, but when it is read aloud it sometimes sounds stiff and literary. I wanted the story to have an immediate impact on the kids, so I adapted Stevenson's tale so that the words would fall easier on the ear. I used as much of his brilliant language as I could in order to retain the original flavor of the story. You are certainly welcome to use my adaptation, but I suggest that, if you wish to add this story to your repertoire, you go back to Stevenson's text and shape a version that is best suited to you.

BILL MOONEY started telling stories back in the early 1960s when he premiered his evening of American frontier humor entitled "Half Horse, Half Alligator" in Vienna, Austria. His recordings with David Holt have twice been nominated for a Grammy. He is the co-author of five books, with two more in the works. He was an actor for many years in New York appearing on and off Broadway, in movies, and on television. During his thirteen-year stint on *All My Children,* he received two national Emmy nominations for his role as Paul Martin.

THE BOTTLE IMP

Keawe was a sailor from Hawaii. One day he found himself in San Francisco, walking around the city, looking at the great houses and thinking, *How happy these people must be! No cares! No worries about money!* Just as he was passing a house—a house smaller than the rest—beautiful like a toy—windows bright like diamonds—an elderly man looked out at him. Truth is, as the man looked out, and Keawe looked in, each one envied the other.

All of a sudden, the old man beckoned.

"Would you like to see my house?"

He led Keawe from cellar to roof. It was beautiful, perfect. Keawe said, "If I lived in a house like this, I'd be laughing all day long."

The old man said, "No reason why you shouldn't have a house like this, even finer. You have some money, I suppose?"

"Fifty dollars. Not enough for a house like this."

"I'm sorry you don't have more. It may give you trouble in the future. But it's yours for fifty dollars."

"The house?"

"No, the bottle. All my fortune, this house and garden, all came out of a bottle."

He took out a round-bellied bottle with a long neck. Keawe could see, through the rainbow colors, something moving inside, like a shadow and a fire.

"Try to break it."

Keawe threw it on the floor, but it jumped back like a ball.

"An imp lives in it. That's the shadow you see moving in there. Any man buys this bottle, the imp is at his command. All he desires—love, fame, money, houses—they're all his as soon as he says the word. Napoleon had this bottle and became the king of the world. Captain Cook had it. He found his way to Hawaii, then he sold the bottle and was killed. Because, once it is sold, its power and protection leave you."

Keawe asked why he was selling it.

"I am growing old. That's one thing the imp can't do—prolong life. One drawback to this bottle: if you die before you sell it, you will burn in hell forever."

"In that case," said Keawe, "I won't touch the thing."

"Dear fellow, just use the power of the imp in moderation. Then sell it to someone else, and finish your life in comfort."

Keawe asked why he was selling the bottle so cheaply.

"Long ago, when the devil first brought it on earth, it was very expensive—millions of dollars. But it can't be sold unless it is sold for less than what was paid for it. Take it from me—if you sell it for as much as you paid for it, back it comes to you like a homing pigeon. The price has kept falling all these centuries. I bought it for only ninety dollars. But when you offer such an unusual bottle so cheaply, people think you're joking. Just remember it must be *coined* money that you sell it for."

Keawe said, "How do I know this is true?"

"Give me your fifty dollars, take the bottle, then wish your fifty dollars back in your pocket. If that doesn't happen, I'll give you back your money."

Keawe handed him the money, took the bottle and said, "Imp of the bottle, I want my fifty dollars back."

There it was, in his pocket again.

The old man said, "Now, good morning to you! and the devil go with you!"

"Hold on," said Keawe, "I don't want any more of this fun. Here, take your bottle back."

"You bought it for less than I paid for it. It is yours. Now get out."

Keawe found himself out on the street with the bottle under his arm. He set it down in the gutter and walked away. Something hit his elbow. The bottle was jammed into his coat pocket. He sold the bottle to a shopkeeper for sixty dollars, but back on board the ship, the bottle was waiting for him in his sea chest.

When Keawe told his mate, Lopaka, about the bottle, Lopaka said, "What will you wish for?"

"I want a beautiful house and garden on the Kona coast, where I was born, flowers in the garden, glass in the windows, with balconies like the King's Palace. I want to live there and make merry with my friends and relatives."

Lopaka said, "Well, if all your wishes come true, I'll buy the bottle from you and get a schooner and go trading through the islands."

When they arrived back in Honolulu, Keawe found that his uncle had suddenly become very rich and then had died mysteriously. All his land and wealth now belonged to Keawe. He thought, *Did the bottle cause this? I imagined my house on my uncle's land. But if uncle died because of my wish, it is evil indeed.*

Keawe was now rich. He built a house on the mountainside, visible to ships. The forest ran up into clouds of rain. Black lava fell in cliffs where the kings of old were buried. There was a garden with every hue of flowers. The house was three stories high with large rooms and balconies and beautifully furnished. It was called *Ka-Hale-Nui*—Bright House. It was better than Keawe dreamed it would be. He was sick with satisfaction.

"The house comes from the devil. I may as well take the good along with the bad. But I'll make no more wishes." And he sold the bottle to Lopaka, who left to make his own wishes.

The years passed. One day, Keawe was riding on the island, and he came upon a beautiful woman bathing in the edge of the sea.

"I thought I knew everyone in this country. How is it I don't know you?"

"I am Kokua, daughter of Kiano, and I have just returned from Oahu. Who are you?"

"Are you married?"

Kokua laughed. "Are you married yourself?"

"I am not, and never thought to be until this hour. But I saw your eyes, which are like the stars, and my heart went to you as swift as a bird. And so now, if you want none of me, say so, and I will go to my own place; but if you think me no worse than any other young man, say so, too, and I'll be stepping to your father's door."

Well, I won't tell you all of the courtship of Keawe and Kokua. Things went fast, but they also went far, and the very thought of Kokua made Keawe sing. He sang everywhere. Eating on his balcony, he sang between bites. His singing startled men on ships. He sang as he went into the bathroom. He sang as he filled the marble tub. He sang as he undressed. Then the singing stopped.

As Keawe undressed, he saw a patch on his flesh like a patch of lichen. He knew what it was: a sickness called leprosy. Now, it's a sad thing for any man to get leprosy. And it would be sad for anyone to leave so beautiful a house and go live on Molokai in the leper colony. But what was that to Keawe, who just yesterday had met his love and won her, and now saw all his hopes shatter like a piece of glass? Never see Kokua again! Never touch her! Never marry her!

In the middle of the night, he remembered the bottle.

The next morning he rode down through the rain and caught the steamer to Honolulu to look for Lopaka. But Lopaka was on an adventure in Pola-Pola with his fine new schooner. Keawe remembered Lopaka's lawyer, who gave him a name. That name gave him another name. And so it went for days, from one name to the next, from one house to the next, until at last he came to a new house on Beritania Street. The owner was a young man, white as a corpse, black about the eyes, the hair shedding from his head. He had the look of a man waiting to be hanged.

The young man reeled against the wall when he found out Keawe had come to buy the bottle.

"What is the price by now?"

"The price? You don't know the price? It has dropped a great deal since your time."

"Well, then I shall have to pay less for it. What did it cost you?"

The young man was white as a sheet.

"Two cents."

"What! Two cents? Why, then, you can only sell it for one. And he who buys it... can never sell it again."

The young man fell to his knees. "For God's sake, buy it! I was insane when I bought it at that price. I had embezzled some money and would have gone to jail! The bottle was my only hope."

Keawe said, "Poor creature, here. Here is the one cent."

As soon as Keawe had the bottle, he breathed his wish to be a clean man. And, sure enough, when he got back to his room, his flesh was whole again. But at the same moment, his soul shrank. He had just one thought now. Not leprosy. Not Kokua. Just the thought that he was now bound to the bottle imp for all eternity, with no better hope than to be a cinder in hell.

He returned to Bright House and married Kokua. When they were together, Keawe's heart was calm, but as soon as he was alone, he began brooding. He heard the flames of hell crackle in the bottomless pit. Kokua was full of song, and went to and fro in Bright House, caroling like a bird. Keawe would listen to her with delight, then would shrink aside to cry and groan about the price he had paid for her.

But eventually, Kokua sang less and less. One day Keawe found her sobbing on the balcony floor and asked what was wrong.

"Oh, Keawe, once your face was bright as the sunrise. But since we married, you have not smiled. What is this cloud I throw upon my husband?"

"Poor Kokua."

Keawe sat down by her side and told her everything.

She said, "You have done this for me? No man can be lost because he loved Kokua. I shall save you. All the world is not American. In France, they have a small coin they call a *centime,* five to the cent, or thereabout. Come, let's go to Tahiti. There we have four *centimes,* three *centimes,* two *centimes,* one *centime*—four possible sales to come and go on, and two of us to push the bargain."

They sailed to Papeete. They hired a house and a fancy carriage and soon became the talk of Tahiti. They began to push the bottle. But it was not so easy to persuade people that great health and untold riches could be theirs for just four *centimes*. Keawe and Kokua had to explain the dangers of the bottle; people either didn't believe them and laughed, or they drew away.

One night Kokua woke to find Keawe gone. She found him, moaning and crying, out under the banana trees, his mouth in the dust. She thought, *How dull I've been. It is he that faces this danger, not I. He did it for my sake. Now I say goodbye to the white steps of heaven. A love for a love, and let mine be the equal of Keawe's. A soul for a soul.*

She dressed and gathered up the *centimes*. The town slept as she walked the streets. She heard an old man coughing in the shadows.

"Sir, will you help a daughter of Hawaii? Let me tell you a story," and she told it from beginning to end. "So, you see, if I offered to buy it, he would refuse. But if you go, he will sell it to you eagerly. I will wait for you here. You buy it for four *centimes,* and I will buy it from you for three."

The old man went in search of Keawe. Kokua stood alone in the street trembling like a frightened child, her spirit dead.

The old man returned. "I left your husband weeping like a child."

He held out the bottle, but Kokua said, "Before you give it to me, old man, ask to be rid of your cough."

"No, I am too near the grave to take a favor from the devil."

"Then here is your money. Give me the bottle."

Kokua walked through the town for a long time. Now all roads were the same, and each one led to hell. Near daylight, she went back to the house. Keawe slept like a child. She lay down beside him, and her misery was so great that she instantly fell into a deep sleep. Later in the day, when Keawe was eating—she couldn't take a bite—he thanked her for saving him. He laughed that the old man was fool enough to buy the bottle. When Kokua replied that maybe he had good reason, Keawe said, "Nonsense! An old fool, I tell you. The bottle was hard enough to sell at four *centimes;* at three it'll be impossible. It's true I bought it for a cent, but that was stupid of me. Whoever has that bottle now will carry it to the pit."

"Oh, Keawe, why do you laugh at the misfortune of another? I would pray for the poor man."

"Heighty-teighty! Kokua, you're not acting like much of a wife. Your husband has just been saved from eternal damnation and you're not happy about it? Seems to me, you're being disloyal! You ought to be ashamed of yourself!"

He stormed out and left Kokua sitting there alone. What chance had she to sell the bottle at two *centimes?* None.

Keawe wandered all over town drinking. He knew in his heart that his wife was right, and the knowledge made him drink even more. Now there was a man drinking with him who had been a bosun on a whaler—and a convict—a man who had a low mind and a foul mouth, a man who loved to drink and see others drunken. Soon there was no more money.

"Here, you! You're rich, or so you've been saying. You have a magic bottle or some foolishness."

"Yes, I'll go back and get some money from my wife."

"Never trust a petticoat with dollars, mate. They're all as false as water. You keep an eye on her."

Keawe thought, *False…yes. Why else should she be so sad about my good luck? I'll show her! I'm not a man to be fooled. I'll catch her in the act!*

He had the bosun wait for him at the corner. When he opened the door to his room, he saw Kokua on the floor wringing her hands, the round-bellied bottle with the long neck in front of her. He was struck dumb. He closed the door softly, then came in again, noisily.

"I've been drinking all day and I've just come back for more money."

This time, the bottle was nowhere to be seen. He went to the chest and took out the money. He looked in the corner where they had kept the bottle. No bottle there. He thought, *She's the one who's bought it.* Then he said, "Kokua, I said some stupid things before. I'm going back to drink with my friends, and I'd take more pleasure in the cup if you'd forgive me." She hugged and kissed him with tears.

At the corner, the bosun was waiting.

"My wife has the bottle, and unless you help me get it back, there can be no more money and no more liquor tonight."

"You're serious about that bottle?"

"Offer my wife these two *centimes* for the bottle. Bring it back here and I will buy it back from you for one. That's the law with this bottle. It must always be sold for less. But not a word that you have come from me."

"Mate, are you making a fool of me?"

"If you doubt me, as soon as you are clear of the house wish for a pocket full of money, or a bottle of the best rum, or what you please, and you will see."

So the bosun left and Keawe waited. It seemed a long time before he heard the drunken voice of the bosun singing in the darkness. He came stumbling into the light. The devil's bottle was buttoned in his coat; in his hand was another bottle, which he drank from.

Keawe said, "You have it. I can see that."

"Hands off! Take a step nearer and I'll smash your mouth. Thought you could make a cat's-paw of me, did you?"

"What do you mean?"

"Mean? This is a pretty good bottle, this is. How I got it for two *centimes,* I can't make out, but I'm sure you won't get it for one."

"You mean you won't sell it?"

"No, sir!"

"But the man who has that bottle goes to hell!"

"I reckon I'm going anyway, and this bottle's the best thing to go with I've struck yet. No, sir! This is my bottle now, and you can go fish for another. Here's to your health, and goodnight to you!"

So off he went down the street, and there the bottle goes out of the story. But Keawe ran to Kokua light as the wind. Great was their joy that night; and great, since then, has been the peace of all their days at Bright House.

Bill Mooney

A WORD FROM THE WISE

Since an important part of this story involves leprosy, a disease that is rarely encountered these days, I make sure before I begin the story that everyone knows what it is and how it affects its victims. I also talk a little bit about leper colonies, particularly the one on Molokai.

The story virtually tells itself. It kicks in fairly early and holds everyone's attention. My only telling tip is that you not get in the way of the story. Simply see the events happening in front of you and describe what you see.

The Kiss of Evil

A Cautionary Tale from Iraq

LORALEE COOLEY

Recommended audience: No younger than sixth grade. Ideal for seventh to twelfth grades and college audiences. This is especially effective in a ghost-story concert setting. The telling time is quite lengthy—for me, about twenty-five minutes.

I first began working on this story to tell it at the Corn Island Storytelling Festival in 1987. At the time, Iraq was just another middle Eastern country. Since then, the location is rather "deja-vu all over again," in the words of Yogi Berra, as Desert Storm and the continuing confrontations with Saddam Hussein frequently bring Iraq into our living rooms

It is one of the strangest and most powerful stories I've ever encountered.

The youngest age group I would recommend this for is probably sixth grade, unless it's a ghost-story festival setting, when the audience is there at their own risk. There are places in the story that elicit giggles—possibly because the audience needs some relief. One place that consistently gets a chuckle is toward the end, just before the denouement, when Abdul and the tongue are having dinner together. Go figure.

LORALEE COOLEY launched her storytelling career in 1977, while living in Casa Grande, Arizona, where she and her husband, Ed, found themselves out of work for a year. She ended up as a storyteller because she discovered it was enjoyable, portable, and legal. During the 1980s, when they were living in Atlanta, Georgia, she was the primary founder of the regional

MIKE ADAMS

Southern Order of Storytellers, now a major storytelling organization. They hosted the 1995 National Storytelling Conference. With the name of her storytelling business as *Storyspinning,* she is now listed on Artist Rosters of both the South Carolina Arts Commission and the Texas Commission on the Arts. She lives in a historic 1915 Arts-and-Crafts house in Pampa, Texas, with her husband and their Standard Poodle.

THE KISS OF EVIL

In the marketplace of the city of Basra, in southern Iraq, sat a beggar, day after day, for all the years of his life. Above his head was posted this inscription:

> HERE IS A MAN WHO FOUND MORE TREASURE THAN HE CAN COUNT, AND MORE KNOWLEDGE THAN HE CAN SPEAK OF.

The notice had been placed above the beggar by the caliph, the ruler of Basra, when the story of the beggar had been told to him. The beggar, given the name of Abdul, could not tell his own story, for he had no tongue; he could not write his story, for he had no arms, and he could not dance his own story, for he had no legs. He could not even think his own story, for he no longer had a mind.

And this is how it all came about.

Abdul lived with his wife and young son at the edge of the city of Basra. He tried to farm the land he had inherited from his father, and his father's father... back for generations. Long years before, the soil had been fertile, but too many years of farming and irrigating with the brackish water of the Euphrates River had poisoned the earth, so that only puny crops grew now... not nearly enough to earn a living on.

And so, for most of the time, Abdul and his friends lamented their fate in the coffee house near-by, where they could spend their time and their frustration telling each other how good things used to be.

One day, a stranger—well-dressed and well-to-do—entered the coffee house. He took note of the poor farmers and ordered the finest of foods as a snack. As the stranger began to eat the fragrant dishes brought to him, Abdul was consumed with envy, and his stomach knotted with hunger as the aroma wafted to the table where he sat with his impoverished neighbors.

The stranger invited the farmers to share in the leftovers—and there was plenty for all. And while they ate together, he regaled them with a story of untold treasure far into the desert, there for the taking—if only someone were brave enough to travel with him to claim it.

"You see," the stranger explained, "most men are ignorant, and fear such things as the jinns—evil spirits—which they believe to lurk in the desert, controlling the dark of night and inhabiting the underground places. But you, Abdul," he continued, fixing his gaze on the one who was listening most intently, "you have the mark of an intelligent man who knows such tales are mere superstitions."

Abdul eagerly agreed, and asked where the treasure could be found.

"I can take you there," the stranger said slyly, fingering his beads of bright blue lapis lazuli.

"No, Abdul," whispered his friends urgently. "Why does he want to take you with him? If the treasure is so wonderful, why does he not go by himself? Don't trust him! He'll leave you to a terrible fate!"

"What are you saying?" Abdul spat back at them. "What sort of manners do you have? We have shared meat and salt with him, and—even though he is a stranger to us—we can trust him now."

He turned to the stranger. "I will go with you."

The journey began quickly. The stranger purchased two camels in the marketplace, and off they went. Abdul did not even get to bid his wife and son goodbye, but his eagerness to find the treasure overcame his loneliness at leaving them.

Through desert and wasteland they traveled—just the two of them. "We want no one else to know of this treasure," the stranger assured Abdul. "They would only try to steal it."

But as they journeyed, Abdul began to feel a deep uneasiness. Something seemed amiss. He watched for signs of evil…and his dreams at night when they camped seemed filled with flames of strange colors.

Just as he was about to turn around and go back to Basra—a pauper still, to face the taunts of his friends—Abdul heard the stranger say: "There it is." And Abdul saw a small hill with an archway at the top made of crumbling stones…stones so massive they could only have been put there by an evil jinn.

Abdul prayed to counteract any evil and dismounted his camel. He walked toward the hill, where he could see a narrow opening between the stones. When he came to it, he could see how the sand had drifted over steps leading down toward a dark, heavy door. A chill shivered over him. He turned back toward his traveling companion…only to see him and the two camels suddenly vanish!

Saying his prayer again, Abdul knew he had no choice but to continue down those steps to the door.

When he reached it, he read, by a strange, sickly glow, the inscription:

> LET THE SEEKER KISS THIS DOOR TO ENTER. THERE, INSIDE,
> WILL BE FOUND MORE TREASURE THAN HE CAN COUNT,
> AND MORE KNOWLEDGE THAN HE CAN SPEAK OF.

As his lips touched the cold metal of the door in the sun-scorched desert, Abdul felt the door swing open to reveal an inner chamber filled with an unearthly, greenish light.

But what else he saw was beyond his wildest imaginings! For, just as the stranger had said, he found treasure of gold and silver, the most glittering precious jewels, diamonds, emeralds, rubies…more than Abdul had any way of carrying away with him! He began to fill his pockets with all he could gather.

Then he spied something else…something his eyes, in the odd green light, had not detected at first: skeletons and corpses of earlier treasure-seekers strewn about the cavern floor. Remnants of these earlier visitors filled his nostrils with the stench of death.

But beyond all of that, he heard a voice—so irresistible, so provocative, compelling him to come nearer.

Then he saw, at the far end of the chamber, away from where he stood amongst the treasure and the carnage, a woman so beautiful, so alluring, that all thought of anything else left his mind. She was sitting on a cache of precious stones, calling him to come to her, holding out her slim, ivory arms to him, clad only in the long, lustrous black hair that fell across her shoulders and over the emeralds and sapphires. Her eyes urged him to approach.

Abdul forgot his wife. He forgot his small son, only now old enough to learn to recite the Koran. He even forgot his pitiful, ruined farmland.

All he wanted was this shining, beautiful woman.

As he took her in his arms—forgetting that only a daughter of the night, the Queen of the Jinns, could be in such a place—she promised him that all the riches and wisdom of the world would be his if he would only kiss her.

Her beauty turned to clammy death as his mouth covered hers. And he felt his own tongue ripped out of his mouth by the woman—the jinn—in a kiss of evil that left a gaping, bloody wound in his throat. Immediately, it was filled by the tongue of the woman-jinn herself, and Abdul stepped back in horror to watch this thing he had been holding dissolve into pools of putrid slime.

He tried to speak holy words aloud, but the tongue flung itself back in his mouth as though to gag him. He tried to scream, but could make no sound. And then the tongue began to laugh.

It was not his voice he heard, not even the voice of the woman-jinn who had so bewitched him. But a voice so evil and so sinister that he clawed at his own mouth to rid himself of it. To no avail.

He flung himself out of the cavern, but he had no idea where to go or how to save himself. The tongue took command. Issuing orders, it gave him directions on how to return to his city of Basra.

When he reached the city gates, his stomach reminded him he had not eaten in several days. The tongue directed him to a fine inn, and ordered the most savory and most expensive dishes on the menu.

But there was no flavor when he tried to eat. The gold and silver he had collected weighed heavy in his pockets: he had enough to pay for everything twice over…but he could not taste any of it. The tongue, however, praised the cook for the delicious meal, as Abdul paid for what he could not enjoy.

Abdul wandered the city he had known so well, hoping that somehow he could make his way back to the edge of Basra where his friends could help him. But when he turned in at their favorite coffee house, the tongue began speaking such unthinkable words about these men until they took to fighting amongst themselves, in danger of killing each other.

Abdul hurried away before the tongue caused more danger. He thought that if he only could make it to his own house, he would be safe with his wife and son.

His wife saw him coming near, and she rushed with welcoming arms to help him inside their home. But before she could even get close to Abdul, the tongue began to pronounce the divorce proclamation: "I divorce thee; I divorce thee; I divorce thee."

Horror-stricken, she stopped cold in her tracks. The marriage was over. She was no longer his wife.

Neighbors crowded round her to console her and watched as Abdul helplessly tried to stop the tongue from talking. Holding his hands over his lips, and trying to keep the tongue still with his teeth, Abdul was a study in despair. His eyes grew wide with fright as he saw his only son come running toward him, as eager as his wife had been to greet him.

But the tongue got free. And, to Abdul's shock, the tongue told the boy in a cold, clear voice to stand on the edge of the well in the center of the village. It was an odd command, and the boy looked at his father in confusion.

Abdul shook his head wildly, gesturing that—no! of course not!—the boy should *not* do this dangerous thing, for the well was deep and there was no railing to protect him from falling in.

But the tongue insisted. And the boy obeyed.

Abdul tried to turn and run, thinking if he could only get the tongue away in time, his son might not come to any harm. But as he bolted and ran, the tongue let forth such a blood-curdling shriek that the boy, startled, lost his balance and fell to his death at the bottom of the well.

With that, Abdul was a lost soul. He wandered throughout the streets of Basra, trying anything he might think of to free himself of this cursed tongue.

Whenever a holy man passed by, Abdul would try to attract his attention so that he might write a note to him, telling of the tongue's evil. But the tongue always threw itself back into his throat to choke him, and he never could succeed.

One day, Abdul and the tongue were having dinner beside the banks of the mighty Euphrates River. To Abdul, the food was as tasteless as sand or dead grass, but the tongue complimented the cook on the fine seasonings of cardamom and rosemary.

As the tongue continued with the flattery, Abdul saw a holy man approaching. Quickly, before the tongue could notice, Abdul wrote of his plight with his finger in the dust.

The holy man stopped, read what Abdul had written, and began to speak a prayer to banish evil spirits. As the holy words were spoken, the tongue began to shiver and flail about in Abdul's mouth, knocking him off-balance and into the murky waters of the Euphrates. The tongue flew out of his mouth, leaving him speechless. In the water, Abdul saw several huge man-eating fish approach him as the blood from his mouth spread. But he could not call out for help.

The holy man leapt into the river to save him, but the damage had been done. Abdul's arms and legs were gone. The fish, not daring to harm the holy man, all swam away.

A doctor was summoned, and Abdul was placed in his care until his wounds healed. But his reason was gone. Since he could not speak or write or move, and had no mind to comprehend, no one knew who he was or what his story was.

When the caliph heard of this poor man's plight, he decreed he should be placed in the market square where all could share their goods with him. It was a blessing to feed a beggar, and Abdul never lacked anything to keep him alive. Fellow beggars held his head to give him water from their own begging cups, drop by drop.

Caravans of fine merchandise passed by him. Merchants left coins of gold and silver. Travelers scattered prayer beads of bright blue lapis lazuli at his feet.

But Abdul was immune to all their gifts.

And above his head was the inscription the caliph had posted to warn others of the dangers Abdul had succumbed to. The bronze plaque read:

> HERE IS A MAN WHO FOUND MORE TREASURE THAN HE CAN COUNT, AND MORE KNOWLEDGE THAN HE CAN SPEAK OF.

A WORD FROM THE WISE

This is not an easy story to tell. Give yourself plenty of time to let it "steep" in your mind and imagination . . . maybe several years. Keep the cultural flavor of the story, but be aware of the universality of the themes. Reading this version aloud many times might be useful; then find a practice audience to tell it too, and discover what sticks in your memory, and what gets left out.

Find your own way to tell the story: some things in my version may not be important to your telling; other things might need more development.

One Wish

A Folktale from Ireland

LIZ WEIR

Recommended audience: This story works well with a wide variety of ages, from children as young as ten to teens and then then to all adults but it's especially popular with senior citizens.

This is an Irish adaptation of a story which is very much an international tale type with variants emanating from several countries. I heard a Jewish version in Israel told to me about Elijah and I have also come across a similar story set in India.

LIZ WEIR is a professional storyteller who works with all age groups, promoting the traditional art for which Ireland is world famous. A children's librarian by training, she now travels the world telling children's stories to adults and children, organizing workshops on storytelling, and speaking at courses for teachers, parents, and librarians. She is also an organizer of the annual Ulster Storytelling Festival and has been a featured teller at the National Storytelling Festival and the St. Louis Festival. Her career has taken her all over her native Ireland as well as England, Scotland, and Wales. Overseas she has told stories in Israel, Canada, Australia, and the United States.

ONE WISH

Long ago, a man and his wife lived on a small farm in County Mayo. The man's parents lived with them and because the land was poor they had very little money. Like every other family, they had known sorrow—the old woman had lost her eyesight and been totally blind for ten years; and though the young couple had wished for a child of their own, in the five years they had been married no child had been born to them.

Despite all the hardships, the young man managed to keep the place going and to keep food on the table for his family, until a blight came on the potato crop and starvation came to their door. He knew it was up to him to save the others and he decided to go to the only place where there was still game to be hunted—the landlord's estate.

Now the landlord was one of the hard ones. He said that anyone caught poaching on his land should be hanged. The young man knew the risk he was taking, but he felt he had no choice. He took an old hatchet, the only weapon he had and crept over the wall into the estate.

He roamed all day searching for something to kill, and as evening fell he cornered a beautiful white deer. As he lifted the hatchet to strike, the deer spoke: "Spare me," it said, "and I will grant you one wish."

The young man nearly collapsed on the spot with fright! "A talking deer? A wish? What nonsense is this?"

But the deer continued. "Listen," it said, "if you kill me you'll be hanged. If you ask for a wish it could save you and your family. Come back tomorrow with your answer. I'll still be here if you decide to kill me."

The young man could not believe what he had heard. He thought the hunger was starting to affect him. He walked home, and the first person he met was his father. He told him about the deer and the chance of a wish and the old man immediately said, "Wish for gold. Gold will solve all our problems."

The young man loved and respected his father, but though he thought about his answer, he decided to discuss it with his mother as well. She listened to his tale and immediately said: "Wish for my eyesight to be restored. That is more precious than gold."

He loved his mother and thought over her answer as well, but he felt he should also discuss it with his wife.

She listened to his tale and immediately said, "Husband, I love your mother and your father, too, but five years now we have been praying for a child of our own. Surely that is the most precious wish of all!"

The poor young man didn't know what to do. He knew that he could only have one wish—which was it to be? He tossed and turned all night long, unable to sleep with the worry of the decision. Should he take a wish at all?

Early the next morning he went out into the estate. There was the white deer, exactly where he'd seen it before.

"Well," said the deer, "have you decided to take a wish?"

"Indeed I have," replied the young man.

"Well, name it, and it shall be granted."

The young man took a deep breath and slowly said, "I wish my mother could see my wife rocking our child in a golden cradle."

And his one wish was granted so that the family lived in comfort and happiness for many years.

A WORD FROM THE WISE

I like to tell this tale in a natural relaxed style, keeping it fairly simple. It is an excellent story to use as a model for workshops and I have heard many wonderful adaptations including one about Santa and his elves told by elementary students! There are versions featuring tigers, unicorns, and even on one memorable occasion a talking frozen chicken! It creates pictures in the mind's eye and as such lends itself to being easily retold. It has a natural flow and can give confidence to beginners. A sure winner!

The Man Who Bought A Dream

A Folktale from Japan

TIMMY ABELL

Recommended audience: Grades 3 and up.

I first came across this story in Richard M. Dorson's *Folk Tales Told Around the World* (University of Chicago Press, 1975). Ten years later it still hadn't let go, so I went back and pulled it out. The story is so full of mystery that its meaning is still growing on me, which is why I like it. There are several unexpected surprises as this story unfolds, and along with its unresolved mystery, I have found that it especially jogs the imaginations of young listeners.

TIMMY ABELL is an entertainer of families. Best known as a musician and songwriter, Timmy has always included storytelling as an integral part of his performances. In his years of touring, he has performed at the National Theater in Washington, D.C., the John F. Kennedy Library in Boston, the Three Apples Storytelling Festival, Alabama Tale Tellin' Festival, Charleston's Piccolo Spoleto, and countless other festivals, schools, and concert halls throughout the eastern United States. Timmy's recordings to date have received national awards for children's media, and his work is featured often on North Carolina Public Television. Timmy grew up in the mountains of western North Carolina where he still lives with his wife, Laura Boosinger, and his three boys.

MIKE GELMAN

THE MAN WHO BOUGHT A DREAM

There was a man once, and he bought a dream. His friend, the one who had dreamed the dream, tried to talk him out of buying it. After all, it was only a dream; why would anyone waste money on something so worthless? But the man was determined to pay his friend so he could have the dream.

Now, the man who bought the dream was very poor. He was always struggling to make ends meet, so when his wife found out that he had spent their precious little bit of money on someone else's dream, she was very upset.

"How could you be so foolish!?" she asked. "What are you thinking? Why would you want to buy someone else's dream?"

"I think this dream could be worth something," her husband replied. "I was watching my friend sleeping, and just as he was waking up, he yawned, and a little bee flew out of his nose. Then he told me he had dreamed about a jar of gold. This jar of gold was buried underneath a nandin bush, and the nandin bush was next to a tall pine tree, which was at the foot of a little mountain in the gardens behind a big mansion. He told me this mansion belongs to the richest man in Osaka, and I really think I have to go there. I had to buy the dream so that I could find my way, so that I could see how to get to the gold."

So the man packed a few things and set off on his journey—even though his wife was still very upset. Osaka was four hundred miles distant, and the journey took many days by foot. It was a difficult journey. He begged for food when he was hungry and slept along the side of the road.

When at last he arrived in Osaka, the man began asking people in the streets to name the richest man in the city. They told him about a man named Kiibe-san and they sent him in the direction of his home. Sure enough, when he came to Kiibe-san's address, he saw a huge mansion. The man who bought the dream was thrilled. He went right up to the house, and when he knocked, a servant came to the door.

"Is this Kiibe-san's house?" the man inquired.

"Yes, it is," the servant replied.

"Well, do you have a little mountain in your back garden?"

"Yes, we have."

"Well, is there a big pine tree by the little mountain?"

"Yes, there is."

The man was getting more excited with every question. "And is there a nandin bush beside the pine tree?"

"Yes, there is."

The man who bought the dream was delighted. He made arrangements with the servant to meet with Kiibe-san over dinner and then stay for the night. During the evening meal, the man told Kiibe-san all about the dream he had bought and all about the jar of gold. "I will share some of the gold with you," he offered Kiibe-san, "if you will have your servants dig up the jar tomorrow."

After everyone was in bed, Kiibe-san kept wondering, "Can this jar of gold really be on my property?" He awakened his servants and told them to begin digging under the nandin bush. Late in the night, they finally came to the top of the jar. Now Kiibe-san was ready to take this gold for himself, but when he opened the jar, a little bee flew out, and the jar was empty. Kiibe-san thought about the man who bought the dream, and he began laughing and laughing. Then he ordered his servants to bury the jar again.

The next morning, the man who bought the dream was very excited. He went out with the servants and began digging under the nandin bush, hoping to find the jar. For the servants, the digging was easier this time, but they said nothing about the night before. When they found the top of the jar, the man who bought the dream yelled with delight. "There it is! This is it!"

Slowly the man who bought the dream uncovered the jar; carefully he removed the top. He could not believe his eyes. The jar was empty!

Now the man who bought the dream didn't know what to do. He felt so foolish having bought this dream that turned out not to be true. His heart broken, his head down, he thanked Kiibe-san and set out on his journey back home. He was so distressed that he even thought of not returning to his wife. How could he face her now? He had spent their last few coins on a worthless dream.

But of course the man who bought the dream had no other place to go, and he knew that he loved his wife no matter how poor they might be. Still, he took a long, long time to get back to his own village.

As he approached his house, he saw his wife through the window. She came running out, hugging him and telling him how happy she was to see him. Now the man was surprised to be welcome, until she told him how, while he was gone, she had heard a little bee in the attic. When she went and opened the attic door, the bee flew out. And then, she said, hundreds and hundreds of gold coins came rolling out of the attic, down into the house, and onto the floor. So many coins had come out of the attic, she told him, that the floor was completely covered with gold.

Now, the man who bought the dream and his wife? They lived happy days all the rest of their lives, and they were never poor again.

A WORD FROM THE WISE

When I tell the story to kids, I sometimes stop just at that dramatic moment when the man who bought the dream is about to open the lid. "What do you think is going to happen?" I ask. They always think that, this time, the man will find gold in the jar; they sense that the man is destined to get the gold, so it deepens the intrigue when they find out the jar is empty. This story begs for discussion after the telling, and it inevitably brings out varying theories on the purpose and identity of the little bee.

The Tale of Delgadina

A Fairy Tale from Chile

LAURA SIMMS

Recommended audience: Grades 1–4.

I first heard the tale of Delgadina from an elderly Chilean woman, the mother of the cook in a restaurant I often went to on Fourth Street in Greenwich Village. She had listened to fairy tales when she was growing up, and she wanted to meet me because I was a storyteller. Wrapped in an embroidered cape, her eyes closed, she told me stories in a back room beside the kitchen. The words mixed in my memory with the delicious spicy smells of Chilean food. The words of the old woman still give me courage: "In the old times the snake was the giver of wealth and rain. He was worshipped and never harmed."

Later, I searched and found a version of the story collected by a retired army general named Manuel Urrea in 1961. I mixed both versions and reconstructed the story for young listeners. I have told this tale to more children than almost any other tale I tell. They love the story of Delgadina and rejoice at her victory.

The roots of this South American fairy tale lie in both the native and colonial Spanish cultures. The tale of kings and queens are familiar to us from European tales, but the magical elements of snake and gold come from the South American mythology, where the snake is sacred. There are ancient tales of holy waters where gods and goddesses arise as huge serpents capable of bringing gold. In the holistic religions of traditional peoples, the saliva of snakes is used for healing.

BOB MARSHAK

Laura Simms, an internationally acclaimed, award-winning storyteller and author, has been telling stories since 1968. She served for seven years as a member of the Board of Directors of the National Storytelling Festival, and in 1985, co-founded the New York City Storytelling Center. She has produced eleven audio- and videocassettes, as well as authored *Rotten Teeth,* which won a Storytelling World Award in 1999. She won the 1999 Sunny Days Award for contribution to children of the world. A frequent contributor to *Parabola* and *Humanity* magazines, Laura lives in New York City where she continues to perform, write, and teach.

THE TALE OF DELGADINA

A little girl named Delgadina found a tiny red snake in the forest near her home. She made a beautiful painted box for the snake and played with him all day. Then at night she slipped the box beneath her bed. In the morning she saw that the snake had grown three times his size. Her mother said, "It is a magic snake. You must care for it."

Every day the snake grew bigger and bigger, until he filled the whole room. Delgadina had no fear of the snake, and the snake did her no harm.

But the snake continued to grow.

One day, Delgadina's mother said, "My daughter, the snake is too big to stay in the house. He must live in the forest."

Delgadina watched the snake slither from the house to the forest. She saw him slide into the mouth of a cave. Every day she visited the snake and fed him. Still the snake grew bigger.

Delgadina's mother said, "My daughter, we are too poor to feed the snake. He will not leave without you sending him away. Perhaps he will be happier to live with other snakes and water creatures."

Sadly, Delgadina called out: "My little red snake!"

The large red snake made his way to the mouth of the cave. "Delgadina, what do you want?" To her surprise, he spoke in a deep and gentle human voice.

"My mother says we are too poor to feed you. She says that you must go and live in the ocean. I will miss you."

"Your mother is right. It is time for me to go. But before I go, let me give you a gift. Take your hands and rub them on my eyes three times."

Delgadina did as the snake bid her do.

"Now, Delgadina, whenever you wash your hands and shake your fingers dry, golden coins will fall from your hands."

Delgadina thanked the snake. She watched him as he slithered gracefully toward the ocean.

Years passed. Because of the snake's gift, Delgadina and her mother grew rich. But they were as generous and as kind as they were wealthy, and they shared their good fortune with anyone who was in need. So all who lived by that forest greatly benefited from the snake's gift.

Not far from Delgadina's house there lived a king who was looking for a queen. He heard about the beautiful girl who could shake gold from her fingers and whose heart was kind. *This young woman would make a good queen,* he thought. But since he did not know Delgadina's family, he wondered how he could meet her.

In the kingdom there lived an old woman who was wicked and jealous. She knew dark magic and hated the wealth-giving snake. When she heard that the king wanted to meet Delgadina, she went to him. "I know Delgadina's mother. If you give me a golden coach with four white horses and a dress of diamonds and pearls, I will bring Delgadina to you."

The king didn't know that she was wicked. Nor did he suspect her use of evil magic. He gladly gave her the golden coach with the white horses and a dress of diamonds and pearls.

Now the old woman had a daughter and she had no intention of marrying Delgadina to the king. She wanted her own bony, ugly daughter, to be queen. So she dressed the wicked girl in the beautiful dress of diamonds and pearls. She sat her in the golden carriage, hid her under a cloak the color of night and drove off to Delgadina's house.

When Delgadina's mother saw the shining carriage with the four white horses approach, she thought it had come from the king's palace. The old woman stopped the carriage and said, "The king would like to marry your daughter."

Delgadina's mother was delighted. Delgadina agreed to the wedding because she had heard that the king excelled in goodness and generosity. When the mother prepared to travel with her daughter, the old woman screeched, "We'll come back for you in a few days."

Lovely Delgadina, dressed in her best gown, climbed into the dark carriage and bid her mother good-bye. The wicked one locked the door, whipped the horses, and rode off as fast as she could in the opposite direction.

Delgadina realized they were not riding toward the king's palace. They were riding up the winding road to the edge of the cliffs that overlooked the sea. As her eyes adjusted to the dark, she noticed in the shadows a bony, ugly girl covered in a black cloak.

Delgadina knocked at the window for the old woman to stop. But the wicked one urged the horses faster and faster until they climbed to the highest cliffs. The old woman stopped the carriage, unlocked the gilded door, took Delgadina by the shoulders, and carried her to the cliff. With her long fingernails she pressed the girl's eyes, and threw her into the sea. Then she drove her own daughter to the royal palace.

Everyone in the kingdom was ready for the wedding. Colorful banners waved in the wind and joyful music played. A great feast had been prepared, and a red rug lay down from the palace to the road. But it was the old woman's nasty daughter who walked on the royal rug.

When the king saw his bride, he was astonished, for he had heard of Delgadina's beauty. But he thought, *If she is truly as kind as I have heard, I will marry her. For true beauty is within and not without. Yet I must know the truth. I will know if she is Delgadina if she can shake gold from her fingers.*

He said to the girl, "Why don't you wash your hands before we get married?"

But the witch's girl was clever. She answered, "I never wash before morning." So the king married her.

By morning, he couldn't stand the sight of her. He watched her wash her hands in hopes that he could prove she was not his true bride. The girl washed her hands and shook her fingers dry. No gold fell from her hands. The king sat back and silently rejoiced. *Good, now I can be rid of her.*

But the clever girl raged, "I spent one night with you, and I lost all my magic." The king was speechless. So he remained wed to the false Delgadina.

The real Delgadina was washed ashore on an island. An old shepherd found her and took her home. Delgadina could not see, and she lay ill for many days.

Delgadina did not tell the shepherd her name or her story, for she was too sad to talk. The old man cared for her, and she did what she could do to be of help to him. But every morning and every evening she went to the shore, stared unseeing in the direction she imagined her mother to be, and sang,

I wish I could go home again
my mother I would see.
For she is very far away,
somewhere across the sea.

One day, as Delgadina heard a sound in the waves, a familiar voice called her name, "Delgadina, I heard your sad song across the sea. Whatever happened to you?"

She reached out to touch the face of her friend. "My little red snake, how glad I am to hear your voice." She told him the story of all that had occurred.

The red snake exclaimed, "I can make you better. Take your hands and rub them on my eyes three times. Now press your hands on your own eyes."

Delgadina did as the snake bid her do.

"Now, Delgadina, lift your hands from your eyes."

When Delgadina lifted her hands, she could see again.

The snake said, "Wash your hands and shake the shepherd a pile of gold to last him his entire life."

Delgadina gladly did as the snake asked. She told the shepherd her tale and bid him goodbye. The shepherd wished her well and thanked her for the gift.

Bright-eyed, Delgadina climbed on the back of the snake. He carried her across the ocean to her mother's home.

When they were reunited, Delgadina and her mother laughed and cried for joy. She told her mother all that had taken place.

Word travels fast, and Delgadina's return was celebrated by everyone whom she had helped. Within weeks, the news reached the king. He wanted to marry her and be rid of his awful bride. He knew, however, how hard it would be to outwit his wife and her mother. He had to prove that she was not Delgadina. He decided to hold a feast in honor of his bony bride. He invited every single person in Chile.

He ordered the cooks to fry the greasiest food. There would be no towels, so all who washed would have to shake their fingers dry. She who shook gold from her hands would be the true Delgadina.

Everyone came to the feast, including Delgadina and her mother. The false bride was pleased to have a party in her honor. All the people, including the soldiers, the guards, the courtiers and the guests, ate greasy food and had to shake their fingers dry when they washed.

When Delgadina shook her hands, gold fell from her fingers.

The king rejoiced. The wicked mother and her scheming daughter were angry. The soldiers were too busy eating to notice.

"Let's get out of here," the wicked one said to her daughter, "and not empty handed." They took the golden carriage, treasures of gold, and the dress of diamonds and pearls. The king saw them leave, but he didn't care. He was glad to be rid of them. The witch and her daughter got into the carriage and rode away.

Happily, the king stamped on the ground three times.

He stamped so hard, the earth shook all the way down to the ocean where the red snake slept. Waking, the snake looked up to see the carriage on the road. He burrowed a hole beneath the earth until he was directly under them. Then he wiggled and turned and twisted and shook and stood straight up, blowing the carriage to bits.

That night Delgadina married the king and became his queen.

From that day forward, whenever they had a problem that they could not solve they stamped on the earth three times and called for the snake. Delgadina placed a small golden crown upon his head and the snake would advise them.

Delgadina and the king and the snake ruled the kingdom with wisdom and wealth and kindness. Because of that, everyone lived happily ever after.

A WORD FROM THE WISE

When telling a fairy tale, the most important thing the storyteller must do is differentiate between oneself (the ordinary person telling the story) and the landscape of the story. The most simple and direct telling is the most potent.

I prompt tellers to not favor any single character but to investigate how they interact. Is is the most difficult character who forces the story to move to its ultimate great ending. Try not to see the witch as only evil, but as the catalyst that causes what is out of balance to come back into balance. The snake is magic; therefore it is both generous and frightening. The girl does not see the snake as an enemy and therefore wins its essential wealth of heart. The gold is a symbol not of material wealth, but of wish fulfillment and abundance.

FAMILY AND COMMUNITY

The Changeling

A Folktale from Ireland

BATT BURNS

Recommended audience: Ages 9–14.

My grandfather, Michael Clifford, had an inexhaustible store of ancient stories, and for me, as a child, the wee folk or fairy people were very real. Right in the middle of his farm was the wonderful fairy fort of Lissaree—an earthen ringfort once surrounded by a ditch full of water—a habitation site of some of the earliest people to come to Ireland. My grandfather often told me that when these forts were abandoned by humans they were immediately taken over by the leprechauns and other wee folk who continue to use them for their nocturnal bouts of merrymaking. He would never dare to cut a tree or remove a stone from this site.

On my way to and from school each day I walked through Lissaree, but as soon as darkness enveloped the McGillycuddy Reeks I wouldn't be seen within a donkey's roar of the ancient fort! Some months ago, I revisited Lissaree to try and recapture a little of the haunting magic which this spot held for me as a child. On that occasion the story of The Changeling became truly alive again after more than fifty years.

BATT BURNS has spent the most of his life in the remote village of Sneem in the mountainous area of southwest Ireland, where he was also born. He is deeply rooted in the tradition of the Irish *seanachie* (storyteller), having lived with his grandfather for more than five years of his early childhood. He has been telling tales for decades but did not become a full-time professional until 1994, when he took part in the National Storytelling Festival in Jonesborough. He has performed at many other major United States festivals, including Corn Island and Timpanogos, and is much sought after for college campus performances. As well as being a regular visitor to Harvard, he is much in demand for Irish organizations throughout the United States His summers are spent in Ireland where he leads unique tours of groups who are interested in Irish tradition.

THE CHANGELING

Life was always tough for the poor sheep farmers who struggled to make a living on the rocky foothills of the McGillycuddy Reeks, and Larry O'Shea was no exception. Himself and his wife of ten years, Kate, lived in a one-room thatched cottage that overlooked the ancient fairy-fort of Lissaree, a place where—according to the old people—a lot of otherworldly activity went on in the darkness of the long winter nights. Few dared to pass the fort after midnight lest they be lured in by the haunting music or be tempted to join in the revelry of the wee folk.

Kate and Larry were childless, and more than anything else on this earth they longed for a child of their very own; but it seemed as if the Good Lord was not going to bless them with such a wonderful gift. Like all of their neighbors, Kate and Larry always went to the holy well of St. Crohane on July 29th and prayed fervently as they circled the well numerous times. Exactly six months later, Kate knew she was going to be a mother. When the baby was eventually born in early September, the joy of this couple knew no bounds. They guarded their bouncing baby boy like gold dust, and each evening when Larry returned from the hill, they would sit on either side of the cradle and dote on their beautiful child.

One dark dreary night in the depths of the very next winter, Kate was suddenly wakened from her sleep by the loud howling of gale outside. Her husband lay snoring beside her. He was unusually tired on that particular night, having spent most of the day on the hill searching for two of his sheep. A tiny flame from a dying ember of burning peat flickered in the hearth and illuminated the sleeping face of the baby in the cradle at the foot of the bed.

Suddenly the bolted door opened with a wailing creak. The swirling wind that blew the remaining embers of the hearth into life revealed two ominous dark figures in the doorway. Kate tried to scream as she stared in terror at a black-cloaked man with a twisted mouth and fiery eyes, but she was so paralyzed with fear that no words came. Right behind him was a weird-looking old hag with tousled hair bearing a sickly misshapen child in her arms. The ugly couple moved toward the fire before the tall man turned his fiery gaze on the cradle. When he moved toward the cradle, Kate fainted and knew no more.

When Kate woke out of her fainting fit, she wakened her husband with a piercing scream. Grabbing him, she shouted at him to light the candle. As soon as he did, it was blown out by the old hag who was still lurking in the darkness by the black wall. The same thing happened a second time, but now it was followed by a mocking hollow laugh that caused Larry to fly into a dark rage. He grabbed hold of the tongs by the fireside to strike the hag, but as he raised his hand, he felt the full force of a blackthorn stick on the back of his head. Now his fury knew no bounds, and he beat the old hag senseless before grabbing her by the hair of the head and throwing her out into the howling gale.

Now he could light his candle in peace, but—the Lord between us and all harm—when they looked in the cradle, they saw a hideous little imp with hair growing all over its face. Their heart-rending cries almost shattered the walls of their humble abode and were carried by the howling winds into the neighboring townlands.

Suddenly, as if from nowhere, a tiny little woman with a red necktie appeared in front of them.

"What is the cause of your grief and lamentation at this unearthly hour of the night when all the world is asleep?"

"Look at the cradle yonder and you will soon see the cause of our distraction," roared Larry.

The strange visitor rushed to the cradle, grabbed up the baby and hugged it as she laughed uncontrollably.

"Your laughter is stranger than our tears. How can you laugh in the midst of our terrible sorrow?" barked Larry.

"I'll tell you why. This is my child which was taken from me earlier tonight. I am one of the fairy folk of Lissaree and my people have admired your child ever since he was born. They have already tried to steal him on two occasions by day, for they want him to fight the fairy wars when he gets older.

Tonight they succeeded in replacing your child with mine. But even though this child looks ugly and misshapen to you, to me he is the most beautiful child ever born. Now I will let you into the secret of how to get your child back."

Larry and Kate moved closer to the fairy woman.

"On the very next moonlight night, go to the fairy fort of Lissaree and take with you three sheaves of corn and some fire. Stand at the entrance to the fort and light the first sheaf. When the fairies appear, threaten to burn the fort. My people cannot stand the power of fire and you can be certain that they will return your child. From then on, you must take great care never to allow him near Lissaree either by day or by night. Tie a nail from a horseshoe around his neck and he will be safe from my people forevermore."

Before they had time to thank her, she had disappeared with the baby. Just after midnight on the next moonlight night, Larry took a flaming torch and three sheaves of corn to the ancient fort. As he stood at the entrance and lit the first sheaf, a small wizened little man with a green jacket and red cap appeared from underneath the fort.

"Why do you trouble us in the middle of our feasting on this beautiful night?"

"I want my child back, or I will burn every tree and bush on this fort and even your chambers underneath so that your people will no longer have a dwelling place," shouted Larry.

Suddenly the old man was gone. There was total silence for some time during which the sheaf burned out. Larry grew impatient and angry.

"I am lighting the second sheaf and I will make this place barren and desolate so that forevermore you will be without a dwelling place."

Great noise and commotion were heard inside the fort, and suddenly a chorus of voices shouted loudly, "Stay your hand! Stay your hand! We cannot stand the power of fire and corn. You can have your child back."

Instantly, the old man reappeared with the child in his arms.

"Take him," said the old man. "You have conquered us with the power of fire and corn. Now that he is yours again, listen well to my advice. When you put him in the cradle tonight, take a red cinder from the fire with the tongs and circle the cradle three times. No more will fairy power be able to reach him."

Larry did as he was instructed and from that night on, his beautiful baby boy grew healthy and strong and was nevermore troubled by the fairy folk of

Lissaree. In return, Larry never allowed anybody to cut a single tree or bush or interfere in any way with the ancient fort.

And so—after midnight, all through the winter—the fairy folk of Lissaree sing, dance, and make merry to the music of the fairy pipes, just as their ancestors have done for thousands of years and, like their ancestors, will do for generations to come.

A WORD FROM THE WISE

It is a pity that some storytellers fight shy of telling tales from a tradition with which they are unfamiliar. In Ireland the tradition of fairies stealing human children is a very old folk belief.

If you like this story, take it and mark it with your own individual stamp. There is no need to try and improvise an Irish accent; rather, absorb the story. Read it several times and then read it aloud until the characters take on reality.

Sweet and Sour Berries

A Folktale from China

LINDA FANG

Recommended audience: PreK, grades K–2, and family audiences that have children of this age group.

When I was growing up in Shanghai, I loved to hear my mother tell stories. Her stories, which were full of adventure and excitement, often involved encounters with highwaymen. I was always scared by those highwaymen who would intercept a traveler, brandish a broadsword, and demand toll for the road.

Nevertheless, in Chinese stories, highwaymen are not necessarily bad people. Many would only rob evil rich people to help the poor and the weak. Others could be men and women who were driven to committing crimes simply because they had no other means to survive.

"Sweet and Sour Berries" is set in the Han Dynasty (206 B.C.-220 A.D.). It came from *Hsiao-chin: Filial Anecdotes,* a collection of ancient Chinese stories.

Although LINDA FANG was born in New Jersey, she grew up in Shanghai. In 1980, she returned to the country of her birth. After completing her graduate studies at Georgetown University, she worked in television for eight years before dedicating herself to storytelling full-time. Linda has performed at many venues, including the Kennedy Center, the Smithsonian, National Theatre, the Corn Island International Storytelling

JAN GILBERT

Festival, Toronto International Storytelling Festival, and the Graz Erzählt International Storytelling Festival in Austria. Her book *The Ch'i-lin Purse,* a collection of ancient Chinese stories, is the winner of the 1996 Storytelling World Tellable Tale Award. In September 1998, Linda won the title of "The National Storyteller of the Year." Linda is also the co-founder of The Washington Storytellers Theatre, an organization dedicated to storytelling for adults.

SWEET AND SOUR BERRIES

Some two thousand years ago, in a village along a river, in a cottage near the woods, lived Tsai Shun and his mother.

Although Tsai Shun was only a little boy, he worked hard to help his mother. Every morning, he fed the chickens, cut firewood, drew water from the well, and lit the stove to make breakfast. The rest of the day he worked in the fields with his mother.

The year Tsai Shun turned eight, there was no rain for several months in the area where he and his mother lived. Nothing grew in the fields. Food became scarce. Starved and worried, Tsai's Shun's mother became ill. She lay in bed most of the time.

One morning, Tsai Shun went to the fields hoping to find some wild cabbage. He returned home disappointed.

As he entered the courtyard, he knew something was wrong. All the chickens were gone. The door of the cottage was wide open, and inside, the tables and chairs were overturned. Clothes, pans, and broken pots were scattered everywhere.

Tsai Shun Found his mother lying on the floor in the bedroom.

"Mama, what happened?" he asked.

"Some highwaymen ransacked our cottage. I tried to stop them but a big man struck me down." Mrs. Tsai choked on her tears as Tsai Shun helped her get back to bed.

Tsai Shun went into the kitchen. He checked the rice jar—not a grain of rice was left. He was very sad because he was hungry, and he knew that his mother was hungry, too.

"Mama," he said, "I am going into the woods to see if I can find any wild berries. If I do, I will bring them home for you."

Tsai Shun took a basket from the kitchen and went into the woods. He did not find any wild berries, so he kept on walking.

Finally he saw some wild berries on a tree. They were dark and shiny. He plucked one and put it in his mouth. It was sweet and juicy. He ate another, and another.[1]

Then he stopped. "Mama is still hungry. I must pick some berries for her." As he was picking, he made up a little song:

One for Mama, one for me!
One for Mama, one for me!

Tsai Shun went home with a basket full of berries. "Mama," he cried as he ran into the cottage. "I brought you some berries!"

Mrs. Tsai sat up slowly. She took a berry and put it in her mouth. It was delicious. She ate one after another, until she was no longer hungry.

"My dear child," she said. "You are so good. I am feeling much better now."

"Mama," said Tsai Shun, "I am going back to the woods tomorrow to pick some more berries. Then we won't have to worry about food for a while."

The next morning, Tsai Shun took two baskets and went into the woods for the second time. But when he came to the tree from which he had picked the berries the day before, he burst into tears. The berries left on it were hardly enough to fill one basket![2]

Then he saw some berries on another tree. They were red. He plucked one and ate it. It was sour![3] *What shall I do?* he said to himself. *There are not enough sweet berries for both of us.*

Then he had an idea. "I will put all the dark black berries in a basket for Mama, and put the red ones in another basket for myself." As he did so, he sang a little song:

Sweet for Mama, sour for me!
Sweet for Mama, sour for me!

When the two baskets were filled, Tsai Shun headed home. *"Sweet for Mama, sour for me; sweet for Mama, sour for me!"* he sang happily as he walked home.

All of a sudden, he was startled by a loud cry.[4] A man dressed in black leapt out of the bushes. He was wearing a black mask. It was a highwayman! "You must pay for using my road!" the man demanded, pointing a knife at Tsai Shun.

Tsai Shun began to cry. "I don't have any money. Please don't kill me!" he begged as he tried to hide the two baskets behind his back.

The man would not listen. "You're lying. What do you have behind your back?"

"Only two baskets of berries," Tsai Shun replied.

"Give me the baskets," the man ordered.[5]

Tsai Shun laid the baskets down before the man.

The man picked up a red berry and put it in his mouth. It was sour! He spat it out. "How can you eat something like this?" he yelled.

Then he picked up a dark black berry and tasted it. It was very sweet. He ate another, and then another.

Tsai Shun began to cry again. "You are eating all my Mama's berries! She is ill. We are hungry. We don't have any food in the house!"

The man stopped eating. "Stop it. Big boys don't cry. I don't believe a word you are saying. If you are hungry, you can't be happy. But you don't look unhappy at all. I heard you singing just now."

"I was singing to remind myself to give all the sweet berries to my mama," said Tsai Shun. "The sour ones are for myself."

"I've never heard of anyone doing something like this," said the man. "Why should I believe you?"

"I am telling the truth," cried Tsai Shun. "I never lie."

The man was silent for a moment, and then he said, "Let me hear you sing the song once more." So Tsai Shun sang again:

Sweet for Mama, sour for me!
Sweet for Mama, sour for me!

A big tear ran down the man's cheek.

"Why are you crying?" asked Tsai Shun. "Big boys don't cry."

"I just thought about my mother," said the man sadly. "I left her many years ago, when I ran away from home." He wiped his eyes with his hand and then pointed to the basket. "You may go home now. Take your berries with you."[6]

Tsai Shun picked up the baskets and ran home. He gave his mother the berries and told her about the man he had met in the forest.

That night, Tsai Shun and his mother were awakened by some footsteps. Somebody was coming to their door! They held their breath as they listened to the rustling sounds outside. But soon the footsteps went away.[7]

Tsai Shun and his mother waited in the dark all night; they could no longer go back to sleep.

The next morning, when Tsai Shun opened the door, a large bag of rice covered the threshhold.[8] A note was attached to the bag. It read,

> I HOPE THIS BAG OF RICE WILL HELP YOU AND YOUR MOTHER GET THROUGH THE HARD TIMES
>
> —YOUR FRIEND FROM THE WOODS

Highwaymen never came to that village again.

A WORD FROM THE WISE

For me this story is a classic example of how you can turn a seemingly simple or even flat story into one that has the elements of humor and suspense and yet not lose its original gentle and heart-warming touches.

The story is so simple that the plot can be told in thirty seconds. But if we allow our imagination to soar, we will discover that there are many places where we can create drama to grab our listeners' attention. The following examples refer to the numbered passages throughout the story:

1. This part can be acted out. The children love to see the little boy enjoying the berries. You can add something like, "Delicious! Wonderful! Great!" while you pretend you are savoring the berries. I always get big laughs when I do that. You can repeat that when the boy's mother savors the berries, too. The children enjoy the repetition.
2. I run like Tsai Shun back to the place where the berry tree was supposed to be and pause. I change my expression from delight to disappointment, and my expression will inform the audience that something is wrong.
3. Make a face when you eat the sour berries. You can even cry aloud, "It's sour!" I always get big laughs for doing that.
4. I usually drop my baskets and let myself half-fall to the floor. You can add something like, "Give me your money!" Even the kids who are not listening will sit up straight and find out what is going on. Then when the bad guy appears, they are all ears.
5. This part is the highlight of the story. I usually act out how reluctant the boy is when he is forced to give up his baskets, moving slowing toward the "man," looking upset and resentful. Once I put the baskets down, I move away from the "man," with my

eyes fixed on "him," and with an angry look on my face. My expressions always make the kids laugh.

6. I always dramatize the man crying. The kids enjoy seeing a "big man" cry. I speak the man's words as if I were crying. I even add sobs between words. The kids are always amused when they see me do that.
7. If the kids are a bit tired, suspense is the best way to perk them up. I try to dramatize Tsai Shun listening to the footsteps in the dark, and the kids may hold their breath or even cover their ears.
8. A surprise was waiting for the boy. I create the suspense by dramatizing the boy listening by the door to make sure that no stranger is around, and then slowly drawing aside the "latch" to open the door. I jump back as the imaginary bag of rice falls over the threshhold. And then I slowly open the bag as if I am afraid to find something bad inside. Instead, I pull out a handful of rice. I change my expression from fear to delight, and then pick up the note. When I read the note, everybody is with me.

There are many more places in the story that you can dramatize. The ones I have mentioned are only the major ones. This is a story that the kids love and remember, if you tell it from your heart.

"ONE FOR MAMA"

A Traditional Chinese Folk Melody

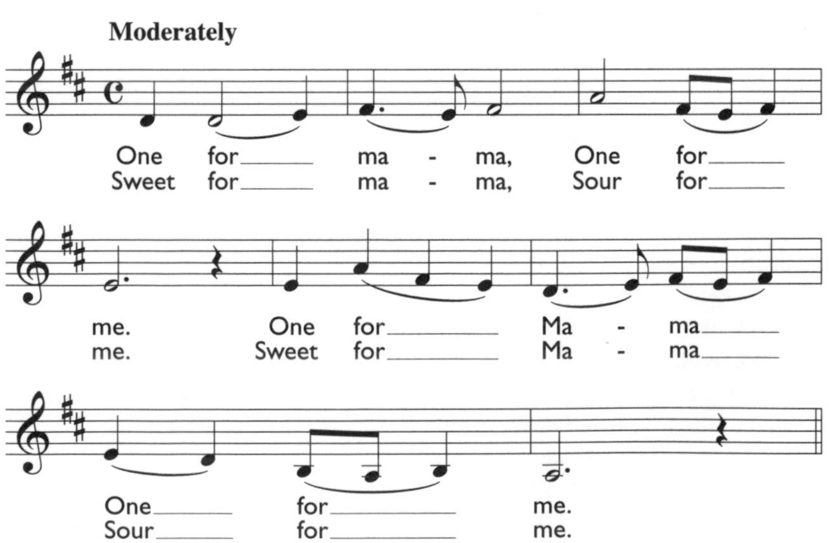

Melody recorded by Chris Patton

The Nixie of the Pond

A Folktale from Germany

DAVID HOLT

Recommended audience: Middle school grades and up.

When I first started telling stories in the 1970s, I decided to read every one of the fairy tales recorded by the Brothers Grimm. There are so many great ones, but "The Nixie of the Pond" is my favorite. It can be told in a very quiet and intimate style. When I first started telling it in concerts, I used a little hand-cranked music box to add some subtle music. Later on, I began to tell it using a flute player who improvised the accompaniment. A few years ago I put together a symphonic storytelling concert with composer David Crowe. Even with sixty-four symphony players going full blast, "The Nixie of the Pond" was not overwhelmed. To me, that is a true test of a great story.

DAVID HOLT is an award-winning musician and storyteller. He is best known for his appearances on The Nashville Network, PBS, and as host of public radio's "Riverwalk." In 1984, Holt was named in *Esquire* magazine's Register of Men and Women Who Are Changing America. He has produced numerous storytelling and music recordings, including Grammy nominee *Grandfather's Greatest Hits* and Grammy Award-winning *Stellaluna.* A native of Garland, Texas, Holt now lives in the western North Carolina mountains.

JIM MAY

THE NIXIE OF THE POND

Once upon a time, there was a miller who had had a pleasant life with all the money and property he needed. But things started to go badly for him, and just as his wealth had increased rapidly, it began to decrease every year until the miller could hardly pay his bills. He worried all the time, and tossed and turned at night.

One morning, he got up before daybreak and went out to walk around the millpond and worry. As the first rays of the sun came up, he heard a rushing sound in the pond, and he turned around and saw a beautiful woman rising slowly out of the water. She had long blond hair which flowed down and covered both sides of her body. He realized that this was the nixie of the millpond. He was frightened, but she spoke to him in her soft voice, and called him by his name, and asked him why he was so sad. She spoke so kindly that he began to tell her that he had been wealthy but now was so poor he didn't know what to do.

"My wife is expecting a baby," he said, "and even the dog and the cat are going to have puppies and kittens at any minute. More mouths to feed!"

"You need not worry," said the nixie. "I can make you richer than you ever were before."

"That would be wonderful," said the miller, "but what do I have to do? What do you want from me?"

"You must simply promise to give me what has been born in your house this very night."

He thought about it. His wife wasn't due for months. Surely, the dog or the cat had had puppies or kittens, and he agreed to give the nixie what was born in his house that night. The nixie sank back down into the water.

He ran back to the house, eager to tell everyone about his good luck. As he opened the door, he was greeted by shouts of congratulations. Seeing his confusion, his neighbors explained excitedly, "While you were out walking, your wife just had a little baby boy!"

The miller stood still, as if struck by lightning. He realized that the nixie had known this and fooled him. He was so ashamed. He didn't know what to say. He could hardly speak. "Why aren't you happy about our little boy?" his wife asked.

He bowed his head and told her what had happened down at the pond. "What good is wealth," he said, "if I lose my only son?"

Not long afterwards, the miller began to make all the money he could use. Everything he did met with success. It wasn't long before he had more money than he had ever had before. He wasn't happy about this, because every time he looked at the millpond he thought about the nixie, and his thoughts turned to the day he would have to give up his son. He never let his son go near the water. "Be careful," he warned, "if you touch the water, she'll reach out and grab you and drag you under and we'll never see you again."

The years passed. Though the boy was very careful, the nixie did not reappear. The miller stopped worrying.

When the boy grew up, he became a hunter for one of the local villages. He met and married a beautiful young woman, and they were very much in love. Once the hunter was tracking a deer, and the animal turned out of the forest and into an open field. The hunter finally killed it with one shot. He didn't realize that he was close to the dangerous millpond, and after he skinned and cleaned the animal, he went to the water to wash his hands. As soon as he dipped his hands in the pond, the nixie rose out of the water. She grabbed him with her soaking wet arms and dragged him down into the water so quickly that only the lapping of the waves above him could be heard.

When evening came and the hunter did not return, his wife grew worried about him and went out to look for him. She followed his tracks far through the forest until they came to the open meadow. When she saw the millpond, and by it the deer and her husband's bow and arrow, she immediately knew what had happened. She called her husband's name but heard no reply. Running to the other side of the pond, she called him again. She began to scream at the nixie to bring him back, but the water's surface remained as calm as a mirror.

She walked around and around the pond—yelling, screaming, cursing, crying—until finally she sank to the ground and fell into a deep sleep. She dreamed that she was climbing up some steep mountain that was covered with briars and thorns. The rain was hitting her in the face, the wind blowing her long hair. But when she reached the peak, everything was calm. Under a blue sky stood a large green meadow covered with flowers. She walked toward a little house at the edge of the meadow, and here in the house sat an old woman with white hair, who invited her in.

At that moment, the young woman woke up. The dream had been so strong that she decided to follow it. At the edge of the forest she found the same steep mountain she had seen in her dreams.

Through wind and rain, she made her way through the briars and brambles until finally she got to the top. It was just as she had dreamed—a beautiful meadow, with a little hut at the edge. She knocked on the door, and a little lady with white hair invited her in.

"Something terrible must have happened for you to have searched me out way up here," the old woman said.

The hunter's wife told her her story, and the old lady said: "I can help you. Here is a golden comb. Wait until the moon is full and then go to the millpond. Sit on the bank and comb your hair. Then when you're finished, set it down on the bank and see what happens."

The woman returned home, and waited and waited. Finally, when the moon was full, she went down to the pond. She combed her hair with the golden comb, put it down on the shore, and stepped back. A wave rose up, swept onto shore, and pulled the comb into the pond. Soon, the water in the center of the pond began to boil and bubble; the surface of the water parted, and she saw the head of her husband rise up in the air. She called to him, but at that moment a second wave rushed over his head and pulled him back under the water. Again, the pond was quiet and peaceful, and only the full moon shone upon it.

The young woman returned home in despair but that night she had the same dream, and again she went up to the woman's hut. This time, the old woman gave her a flute, and said:

"When the moon is full, play this flute on the edge of the pond. Put it by the water and see what happens."

At last, the moon grew full. She took the flute to the water and began to play a sad song. When she was finished, she put the flute down at the edge of the water, and a wave rose up and pulled it back into the water. Out in the center of the pond, the water began boiling and bubbling and gurgling, and her husband began to rise up out of the water. She called to him. Half of his body was out of the water. He reached out to her, but just as he did, a huge wave came over his head and dragged him back under.

It's no use, she thought. Once again, she returned home, but that very night she had the same dream for the third time. When she followed it, the old woman gave her a little golden spinning wheel, and said:

"When the moon is full, sit on the bank and spin until the spool is full of thread. Place the spinning wheel near the water and see what happens."

The young woman did exactly as she was told. When the moon was full, she spun until the spool was full of thread and then put the spinning wheel down by the water. No sooner had she put it down by the shore than the water bubbled from the depths more violently than ever before, and a powerful wave rushed onto the shore and carried the spinning wheel away with it. Soon after, the center of the pond bubbled and gurgled, and the entire body of her husband rose up like a water geyser. She called out to him, he called out to her. As he reached out to her, she ran in the water, and grabbing his arm, pulled him to shore. They began to run through the forest as fast as they could.

They had only gone a short distance when the entire millpond rose up in one giant, horrible wave and smashed through the fields, tearing out trees and everything that was in its path. They could see they were just about to die as the water rose up into one huge wave to overtake them. In the last instant, the wife called out to the old woman to help them, and at that very moment they were transformed—she into a toad, and he into a frog.

When the wave hit them they were carried by the water far, far apart from each other. After the flood had run its course, and both the toad and the frog had touched down on dry land, they each turned back into their human form. Neither of them knew where the other one was. The water had carried them far, far apart. They were among strange people in a strange land and had no idea how to get back home.

High mountains and deep valleys lay between them, and, as luck would have it, in order to earn a living, they both herded sheep in their new lands. For many years, they drove their flocks through their fields and over the mountains and were full of sadness and longing.

One spring day, the huntsman was driving his flock and saw another shepherd on a distant mountain slope. Since he rarely got to see another human being, he began to drive his sheep in that direction. They came together in the valley, and though they didn't recognize each other, they were glad to have companionship in such a lonely place. For several days, they drove their flocks side by side. They didn't speak much but felt comforted.

One evening, when the moon was full and the sheep had gone to sleep for the night, the shepherd took a flute out of his pocket and began to play a beautiful but sad tune. When he finished, he noticed that the sherpherdess was weeping.

"Why are you crying?" he asked her.

"Well," she answered, "the full moon was shining just like this when I played that tune on a flute and the head of my husband rose out of the water."

He looked at her as if a veil had fallen from his eyes, and he recognized his wife. Then she looked at him, and when the light of the moon fell on his face, she recognized him as well. They fell into each other's arms, and no one even need ask if they lived happily ever after.

And from that day to this, no one has ever seen the nixie of the millpond again.

A WORD FROM THE WISE

Like most good fairy tales, this story works on many levels. I feel it is best told to older children and adults. Most adults have been through many changes themselves and relate to the complexity and difficulty of the relationship in this tale. I will warn you, "The Nixie of the Pond" is not easy to tell because the audience must listen closely and be engaged. But the story will reward your efforts. It works best later in a storytelling program, after the audience has settled down and relaxed.

It takes about twelve to fifteen minutes when I tell it. No theatrics are needed. Don't make this one overly dramatic and especially not phony. This is one of those stories that can't be completely explained but rather is felt on some deep level. If you are absorbed in the tale while you are telling it—focused, clear, and sincere—the audience will be as well.

Taen-awa

A Folktale from Scotland

DAVID HOLT from DUNCAN WILLIAMSON

Recommended audience: Grade 3 through adult.

Some of the storytelling highlights of my life have taken place in Duncan Williamson's living room in Bamullo, Scotland. With the coal burning in the fireplace and a bottle of whiskey passing from hand to hand, when Duncan slides out of his chair and sits on the floor, you knew a story was coming. That's the way he had always heard them, sitting on the ground around the fire in a travelers' tent. He comes from a long line of nomadic tinsmiths, pipers, and storytellers. He knows hundreds of old tales.

As Duncan starts telling a story, he looks his listeners in the eye. He reaches out and touches them to make a special point. He inhabits each character with a quiet intensity. You know you are experiencing the real thing... as stories have been told by the masters from the beginning of time.

DAVID HOLT, an award-winning musician and storyteller, is best known for his appearances on The Nashville Network, PBS, and as host of public radio's "Riverwalk." In 1984, Holt was named in *Esquire* magazine's Register of Men and Women Who Are Changing America. He has produced numerous storytelling and music recordings, including Grammy nominee *Grandfather's Greatest Hits* and Grammy Award-winning *Stellaluna.* A native of Garland, Texas, Holt now lives in the western North Carolina mountains.

IRENE YOUNG

TAEN-AWA

There once lived a young farmer and his wife in the west Highlands of Scotland. They were just a young couple and worked hard. More than anything they wanted a baby.

At last, they were blessed with a beautiful baby boy. He was the best little baby. He just laughed and cooed and was as happy as he could be.

One day the farmer and his wife went up to cut hay in the field. They took the baby in a cradle and put him under the shade of a tree. They hadn't been working long when the child began to cry. This was odd because the baby hardly ever cried. The mother went over to see what was wrong—maybe an ant was biting it or a pin sticking it. She couldn't find anything wrong so she said to her husband, "I am going to take the baby to the house and feed and change it and see if it will stop crying."

But no matter what she did, the baby would not stop. It kept crying until the clock struck midnight—and suddenly it stopped. But at six o'clock in the morning it started up again.

No matter what they did, the baby kept crying from six every morning to midnight—day in and day out. It gave them no peace.

This went on for weeks until the parents were about to go out of their minds. One day their friend John, the postman, stopped by to tell them about the market day in the village and to see the new baby. "Oh, John," they said, "we would love to go to market but the baby is crying all the time, and we couldn't ask anyone to take care of it while we were gone."

John said, "I have had eight children myself. Let me have a look at the child." John walked over and pulled back the cover. When the postman took one look at the baby, he could see the skin was shallow and dark and wrinkled. It looked like an old man.

He didn't say anything to the young couple, but he said to himself, "This is not a baby, this is something strange. I've heard stories before about how fairies take children away. I wonder if that has happened here."

He said to the couple, "Don't worry about the baby. I will watch the child. Today is my day off, so I will take care of him if you want to go to the market."

They said, "We couldn't ask you to do that with the baby crying all the time."

John said, "Don't worry. With eight children I can handle anything. The crying won't bother me. I will rock the cradle and take care of him until you come back."

The young couple thanked John over and over, then saddled up the horse and rode off over the hill.

As the horse disappeared in the distance and the old postman sat rocking the cradle, the baby started to sit up. He looked right at John and said, "Are they gone yet?"

John was stunned. "Are you talking to me?"

"You see anybody else here? Are they gone yet?"

John said, "Yes, they've just gone over the hill."

"Good," said the baby. "Get the whiskey."

"What?" said John.

"Get the whiskey. Get a glass for yourself. I know you like a little whiskey too."

John went to the cabinet and got the bottle and two glasses and gave them to the baby. He poured one for John and a glass for himself and drank it down in one gulp. Then he poured himself another glass and said, "John, where can we meet some girls?"

"There are no girls out here," John said. "We are way out in the Highlands."

The baby crawled out of the cradle and waddled over to the fireplace and sat down, looking in to the fire. He said, "John, do you like music?"

"Well, I guess everybody in Scotland loves music," said John.

"Good," said the baby. "Go get a cornstalk and bring it to me." So John went out to the corncrib, found a cornstalk, and took it in to the baby. The baby broke off the cornstalk at both ends until it was about a foot long. He got the poker from the fireplace and put it in the fire until it was red hot. He burned holes in the cornstalk with the poker, making himself a little flute. He sat there cross-legged on the floor and played jigs and reels that John had never heard before.

John looked at him and raised an eyebrow. "You're no baby." But the baby just looked at him and said, "Drink up," and continued to play.

All of a sudden the baby stopped playing and said, "I think I hear them coming."

John looked up and could see the parents riding over the hill and said, "No, I don't hear anyone." He wanted the young couple to see the baby acting this way.

"You're lying, John," the baby said. He threw the flute into the fire, waddled over to the crib and climbed in. Just as the parents came through the door, he pulled the cover around himself and started crying.

They said, "We are sorry to leave you so long with the baby. You must have suffered with him crying all the time."

John pulled them aside. "Come here a minute," he whispered. He took them in the other room and told them what had happened. He said, "That is not your baby in the cradle. That's a taen-awa."

"A what?" said the mother. "What is a taen-awa?"

"The fairies have taken your baby and put something else in its place, a taen-awa. It is not your baby, and the quicker we get rid of him the better."

"What can we do?" said the mother.

"At midnight, when he stops crying, you have to take a new shawl and wrap him tightly in it and throw him in the river, over the waterfall."

The young couple said, "We couldn't do that to our baby or anyone else's, no matter how badly it was acting."

"I tell you, it is not a baby, it is a taen-awa," said John. He finally convinced the couple that something had to be done. So at midnight, when the baby stopped crying, they put its arms by its side and wrapped it tightly in the new shawl. Then they made their way in the darkness to the river's edge at the top of the waterfall.

The farmer's wife was very upset to throw even the poorest kind of baby into the waterfall, but she realized the old postman knew what he was doing. She took courage and threw the baby into the river. It was swept over the waterfall.

When it hit the water, the shawl flew open and there stood an little ugly old man on top of the water. He shook his fist at them and said, "If I knew you were going to do this to me, I would have done worse things to you when I had the chance." And then he disappeared.

The farmer and his wife were very upset as they started to walk back to the house. They were glad to be rid of the taen-awa but wanted their baby back. As they walked up to the door, they heard a little noise inside. When they went in and looked in the cradle, there was their little baby and he was laughing and cooing and just as happy as he could be.

A WORD FROM THE WISE

This tale is an unusual story... mysterious as well as humorous. Everyone is intrigued by this talking, whiskey-drinking baby. When Duncan tells it, the baby's voice sounds like an adult whisper. When I tell it, I give the baby a very gruff, gravelly, adult voice... like some old salty sea captain or perhaps the leader of a motorcycle gang. The kids love this gnarly little baby; surprisingly, I have never had anyone complain that he drinks whiskey.

I have tried putting music in the story, playing Scottish tunes on a tin whistle when the baby starts to play. Interestingly, it didn't add a thing. In fact, it might have broken up the images for the listener. I have found it effective, though, to use a musical coda after the story ends to give the audience a chance to digest this weird little tale.

You don't have to jump around or otherwise "overtell" this story. Just give it a straightforward telling with a personal twist on the baby's personality. The story will work on its own.

Mary and the Seal

A Folktale from Scotland

DUNCAN WILLIAMSON

Recommended audience: Age 13 to adult.

This is a Gaelic tale that was told to me a long time ago by an old crofting (farming) friend of mine from the West Coast of Scotland. It was told to me when I was only about fifteen years of age. I was stone-dyking in Argyll at Auchindrain with a dry stone mason I sometimes worked with and began telling him a few traveling tales. One rainy day, he said, "You know, Duncan, I tell stories, too." "Tell me one," I said. "Oh, I can't tell it in Gaelic, but I'll tell it to you in the best English I know." I can still hear his voice in my ears. It's still there after maybe forty years. Every little detail is imprinted in my memory. When I tell the story I try to get as close as possible to the way he spoke it. This is the story he told me. I hope you enjoy it.

DUNCAN WILLIAMSON is one of Scotland's foremost storytellers. Born near Loch Fyne, the seventh of sixteen children, he left his family when he was fifteen to work in Perthshire. As one of Scotland's Travelling people, Duncan roamed the countryside doing itinerant work—farming and handicrafts—until he met his second wife, an ethnographer. They settled in Fife in 1980 and together deposited his knowledge of three hundred traditional tales into the School of Scottish Studies Archives in Edinburgh; thus his second career was launched.

DAVID HOLT

The wealth of experiences he brought to his telling (he has been a handler of horses, a field worker, and "done everything there is to do on the road") have made him beloved of festival audiences from Israel to Jonesborough and many places in-between. Duncan's festival repertoire now includes many international stories collected in his travels, but his vast knowledge of Scots culture is evident in his books of folktales. He now lives in Balmullo, where is regularly hosts ceilidhs for area storytellers and entertains guests from around the world. He continues to travel, delighting audiences everywhere with his traditional tales.

MARY AND THE SEAL

A long time ago on the West Coast of Scotland there was an old crofting man by the name of Angus who lived by the seaside. He and his wife, Margaret, had only a small croft as well as a small boat and a net. There was not much work to be done in their hard stony croft in those days, so he spent a lot of time fishing. The biggest thing in their lives was their daughter, Mary. She was a beautiful girl and their only child. They loved her dearly.

Even though she was only a child, Mary worked hard helping her parents. Every morning her father would get up early and go out to sea to set his nets. Mary used to go with him and help him lift his nets and collect the fish. She would keep out a few to give to her mother and the rest they took into the village and sold. Her father and mother were so proud of Mary because she was such a good worker, as well as being a quiet and tender little girl.

The years passed and Mary grew up to become the most beautiful girl in the village. Now, I want you to know this village was small—the kind of place where everyone knows everyone else's business—just a post office, a hotel, a grocery, and a few houses. Angus had a cousin by the name of Lachland who also lived by the sea just a short way from Angus's house. Mary loved her Uncle Lachy—who had never married—and often went to visit him.

When she was sixteen or seventeen, Mary started borrowing her father's boat and rowing out to a little island in the middle of the sea-loch that lay about half a mile from where they stayed—a small island of about three acres with no trees, just a lot of rocks and a few bushes. She spent a lot of her time there. Her father and mother never paid any attention to how long Mary stayed there because her spare time was her own. When her work was finished, she could do what she liked.

Until one day.

Her mother walked down to the local shop to buy groceries for the weekend. As she bent over to look for some money in her handbag, she overheard two old women nattering to each other. They were busy talking about Mary.

"Isn't it terrible," one of them said. "She's such a beautiful lassie, but dear! dear! there's something queer going on. She never comes to any of the ceilidhs.* Never comes and has a wee timey when our children have their shows at school. All she wants to do, they tell me, is row out to that lonely little island and spend all her time there. And her mother and father are such decent people... even her Uncle Lachy gets upset!"

This was the first time Mary's mother had heard such talk and it upset her very much. She packed up her bag and walked back home. Her husband, Angus, sitting by the fire smoking his pipe, could see that something was bothering her.

"What's the trouble, Margaret?"

"Oh, the wagging tongues of the village are at it again."

"What are you talking about, woman?"

"Your daughter."

"What about my daughter? Don't we have the kindest, the cleverest, the most beautiful daughter in the whole place! What's the trouble?"

His wife told him what she had heard in the village about Mary spending her time on the island rather than going to the parties and dances.

"Well, woman, what's wrong with that? Would you have her gallivanting down in the village, skylarking around with some young man and maybe destroying herself by bringing back a baby to you that you didn't even want—would you enjoy that better? The girl's doing no harm, woman! What's the problem?"

She said, "Angus, there's something going on out there, and I want the truth. She's been going out there five years. She should spend more time with people. I want to know why Mary is so unsociable."

"Och!" he said. "Woman you're worse than those tongue-waggers in the village. She's probably washing her feet out there or reading a book or something. What harm could she do? She needs a little spare time for herself."

She said, "I want you to find out what's going on out there. The next time she goes to the island, borrow your cousin Lachy's boat and follow her. Find out what she's doing so my mind can be at peace."

* ceilidh (kay-lee): celebration featuring story and song.

Well, they argued for the rest of the night, but Angus had never in his life won an argument with his wife.

The next morning, Mary came down for breakfast. "Good morning, Mummy. Good morning, Daddy. Are you going fishing this beautiful morning?"

"No, Mary," he said. "The tide is high and the nets are well-set, and I can see the floats are not sunk yet. I'll just stay here and have a smoke."

"Father, dear, can I borrow the boat?"

"Of course, my dear. You don't need to ask me. Help yourself to the boat."

Mary got in the boat and rowed herself to the little island.

As soon as she was off, her mother said to Angus, "Look, would you relieve my mind for me? Would you go down and borrow Lachy's boat and row out to the island and see what Mary does out there? It'll put my mind at rest."

"Och, dashit, woman! To keep you happy, I'll go! But it's only a waste of time," Angus grumbled.

So he walked down; it was only about two hundred yards down to Lachy's cottage. He was sitting by the fire. He'd never married; their fathers had been brothers. Lachy was an old retired seaman and he always liked to keep a boat. He had the same kind of boat as Angus.

"Well, it's yourself, Angus!" he said. "Come away in. And come you, sit down and we'll have a wee dram."

"No," he said. "I'm not here for a dram."

"Well, what sent you down?"

"I was wondering if you would let be borrow your boat for a few minutes?"

"Well, what's the trouble? What's wrong with your own boat?"

"Och," Angus said. "Mary's using it."

"Och, that's Mary off on her gallivant to the island again," Lachy said. "You've been listening to the tongue-waggers in the village and now you want to follow the lassie and see what she's doing. If I were you I would leave her alone. Come on, sit down and have a dram with me and forget about it."

But old Angus was persistent, "I want to borrow your boat."

"Well," said Lachy, "take the dashit thing and away you go!"

Angus rowed across to the island and there was his own boat beached. He pulled his cousin Lachy's boat up beside it. Then he followed a path—it was well-worn because Mary had walked up this way many times—up over a little knoll. There he saw some rocks and a few bushes, and down at the back of the island a small kind of valley-shaped place that let out to the sea. There he saw a beach, and on the beach was a large rock. And beside the rock was a wee green patch.

Old Angus came walking up, taking his time—looked all around and looked all around. There were a few seagulls flying around and a few birds wading along the beach because the tide was on the ebb. And he heard the laughing coming on. Giggling and laughing—this was Mary, carrying on.

As he came up over the knoll, he looked down. Here was Mary with a large seal, a gray seal. And they were having the greatest fun you've ever seen. They were wrestling in the sand, carrying on and laughing. The seal was grunting and Mary was flinging her arms around the seal.

Angus sat down and watched them for a wee while. He said to himself, *Och, I'm sure she's doing no harm, it's only a seal. And her mother was so worried about it. She's enjoying herself; probably she's reared it up from a pup and she comes over to feed it, and I'm sure it won't do her any harm. She's better playing with a seal than carrying on with a young man, as far as I'm concerned!*

So he takes Lachy's boat and rows home.

His wife, Margaret, is waiting for him.

"You're home, Angus."

"Aye, I'm home," he said. "Margaret, I'm home. And thanks be praised to God I am home!"

"Did you see Mary?"

"Of course," he said. "I saw Mary. She's out on the island."

"And what is she doing? Is she sitting—what is she doing?"

"She's enjoying herself."

Old Margaret said, "What way is she enjoying herself—is she wading on the beach or something?"

"No," he said, "she's not wading on the beach."

"Is she reading?"

"No, she's not reading," he said. "She's playing with a seal."

"What did you say?"

He said, "She's playing. She has the best company in the world and she's enjoying herself. She's playing with a seal—a large gray seal. They're having great fun and I left them to it and didn't interfere."

Old Margaret's face took on a terrible look. "That's it! I knew there was something strange going on! Mary's enchanted. It's one of the sea-people that's taken over. Your daughter is finished—ruined forevermore. I've heard stories from my grandmother how the sea-people take over a person and take them away. They're never seen again. She's enchanted. What kind of seal was it?"

He said, "A gray seal."

"That's not a common seal. It's one of the sea-folk, and if you don't get rid of that beast, you'll never see your daughter again."

"What do you mean 'get rid of it'? I couldn't interfere. It's Mary's pet."

"I don't care it it's Mary's pet or no," she said. "Tomorrow morning, I'll keep Mary here. I want you to take your gun and go out and shoot that seal and destroy it forevermore."

"Me, is it? Go out there and shoot the pet me daughter's been playing with maybe for years? You must be crazy and out of your mind."

"No, Angus, if you want to see your daughter again, you'd better listen to me."

"I've listened to you too many times. I just can't do that."

"You'll do it tomorrow if you want to see your daughter again."

Well, the argument went on, and they argued and argued, and finally old Margaret won. Angus agreed he would go out in the morning and shoot the seal, even though he felt very sad about it.

When Mary came home that evening, she was so radiant—so bright and happy. She came in and kissed her daddy and mummy. She had a cup of tea and asked Mummy and Daddy if they needed anything or wanted anything done. When they said no, she went up to bed.

The next morning Angus got up early. Before he even had any breakfast, he took his gun and loaded it. He rowed out to the island and beached the boat. Then he walked up the path, the way Mary usually went, over the little hillock, down the little path to the little green patch beside the bare rock. Sure enough, sitting there sunning himself in the morning sun was the seal.

Meanwhile, when Mary got up she came downstairs for breakfast. Her mother turned and said, "You know, Mary, you've been neglecting the cow's byre. I want it scraped and whitewashed. The cow needs a clean place."

Mary said, "Sure, Mother, I'll do that for you."

Back on the island, Angus crept up as close as he could to the seal. He raised his gun and fired. When the shot hit the seal, it reared up...and fell. Then it crawled, made its way into the sea, hobbled its way into the water and disappeared.

As Angus stood there, a queer feeling came over him, a sadness. He sat down and put the gun beside him. He sat there a long time and looked at the gun. He felt that he had done something terrible, as if he had killed someone he loved dearly—as if he had shot his wife or his daughter.

Finally, he picked up the gun and walked back to the boat. He felt so sick he could barely walk. He put the gun in the boat. He sat for a while before he could row back home. He had the queerest sensation: a feeling of loss was within him, a terrible feeling of loss—that something he had done could never be undone. He could hardly row the boat. When he got back to the mainland, he tied up his boat, picked up the gun, and put it back in the cupboard.

His old woman, Margaret, came in and said, "Did you get the seal?"

"Yes, woman, I got the seal."

"What's the matter with you, old man? You don't look well."

"I don't feel well either. I shot the seal. Maybe now you'll be satisfied. Maybe now we'll have some peace in the house. But I don't feel very well about it."

"Och, forget about it. It's only a seal!"

"No, woman, I feel terrible. I've done something wrong and you forced me to it. I hope in the future that you'll be sorry for it."

Just then, Mary came in from working on the cow's byre. She came over and stroked her father's head. "Aren't you feeling well, father?"

"Oh," he said, "I'm feeling fine, Mary. I'm just not... just... what I should be."

The mother tried to hide her face in case Mary could see something that would give her away.

"Well," said Mary, "Father, are you ready to go out and lift the nets?"

"Mary, to tell you the truth, I don't think the outgoing tide will be for a while yet. No, I think I'll sit here and have a smoke."

"Mother," she said, " are you needing anything else done?"

"No, Mary, we don't need anything else."

Now they tried to be as canny* with her as possible. They didn't want to upset her in any way.

Mary said, "Well, after I milk the cow, Father, would it be all right if I take the boat?"

"Och, yes, daughter, go ahead and help yourself to the boat. I'm sure you can have the boat any time. You don't need to ask me for the boat. Just take it whenever you feel like it."

So Mary milked the cow, brought in the milk and set the basins for the cream—she did everything that was needing to be done. "Goodbye, Mother," she said. "I'll see you in a while. I'm just going off for a while to be by myself—I'll be back before very long."

"There she goes again!" Her mother remarked when the door closed behind Mary. "If you tell me it's true, she'll be home sadder and wiser."

*canny: careful

But old Angus never said a word. He just sat and smoked his pipe. He still felt the lump in his heart. He didn't want to get up, just wanted to sit. He had this great terrible feeling of loss.

So Mary rowed the boat over to the island. And her father sat by the fire and he smoked and he smoked and he smoked. Margaret called him for dinner and the day passed, but Mary didn't return. Evening came, but Mary didn't return.

Her mother began to get worried. "Angus, has Mary come home? It'll soon be time for milking the cow again."

"No," he said, "Mary has never come."

"Perhaps she... would you go down and see if the boat's tied up? Maybe she walked down to the village."

Angus went out but there was no sign of the boat.

"No, no boat..." he told his wife.

"Well, she's not home. If the boat's not home, she's not home. I fear something's happened to her, Angus. You'll have to go and see what. You'll have to go out to the island. Go get Lachy's boat and go out to the island and see."

So Angus went down, just walked down and took Lachy's boat—never asked permission—just untied the rope and jumped into the boat. He was so upset, he didn't even worry what might happen. He rowed out to the island, and there was Mary's boat. He pulled the boat in beside Mary's and walked up the path, over the little hillock, down by the big rock to the little bay and the green patch beside the big rock, and walked right down to where he saw the seal.

He looked.

The side of the rock was splattered with the blood where he had shot the seal.

He walked around the whole island, which wasn't very big, walked the whole island round—all he saw were a few spots of blood. Nowhere did he find Mary.

Mary had completely disappeared. There wasn't a sign of her, not even a footprint. He walked around once, he walked around twice, and he walked round a third time; every tree, every bush, every rock he searched, but Mary was gone.

He felt so sad.

"What could happen to Mary, my poor wee Mary, what happened to her?"

When he came back once again to the rock where he had shot the seal, he looked out to sea. The tide was on the ebb. He stood looking for a long while. The blood on the rock was drying in the sun. When he looked out to sea again, all in a moment, up came two seals, two gray seals, coming up right out of the water, barely twenty-five yards from where he stood. They looked at him, directly at him. Then they disappeared back down in the water. And he had this queer feeling that he was never going to see Mary anymore.

So he took his boat and rowed home, just the one boat, took his own boat, left Lachy's boat on the island. He tied up his boat, walked into his house, and sat down beside the fire. His wife, Margaret, came to him.

"Did you see Mary?"

"No," he said. "I never saw Mary. I never saw her. I searched the entire island for Mary and Mary is gone. And look, between you and me, she is gone forever. We'll never see Mary again."

And they waited. And they waited. And they waited for the entire days of their lives, but Mary never returned.

And that is the end of my tale.

A WORD FROM THE WISE

This is a great tale for teenagers or parents of teenagers. Anyone aged thirteen to adult will find a lot to think about in this story. It is a deep story appropriate for special situations where your audience is with you and ready to go to a more profound level. It will work best later in a program when your listeners are settled in and know they can trust you.

Your audience needs to know that this is a story from Scotland. The more background you can give them, the better. There is a wonderful book, *The Horsieman* by Duncan Williamson (Edinburgh: Canongate Press, 1994) in which Duncan tells about his life as a Traveler. It is full of fascinating material that would help set the stage for this tale. Unless you are Scottish, do not use an accent. This story is too deep for affectations; it requires subtlety and honesty.

When Duncan tells this story he makes the voices of each character very real and focused. The entire tale is told with a quiet intensity. The listener feels sympathetic to all the people in the family. No one is the villain. Duncan makes the conversations between the characters as close to real life as possible, and relates a great deal of how the characters are feeling with his eyes. He never tries to make the telling scary or weird. For many folks in Scotland a seal person is within the realm of possibility. That reality gives the story even more power. (Another great book on selkies is *The People of the Sea* by David Thomson [Edinburgh: Conongate Classics, 1996].)

One final thought. This story will leave the audience in a very thoughtful, almost sad mood. Give them a moment to think after it is done, either with a quiet tune if you are musical or just a little silence. Plan out how you are going to follow it up. Lift the audience up to the next story gently.

—DH

BENEDICTION

The Ruby

A Parable from the Hindu Tradition

JIM MAY

Recommended audience: Adult audiences, at end of program.

I have heard many versions of this traditional story over the years. It comes to us from the Hindu tradition. The old man is a *sannyasi,* one who has given up everything in order to live a simple life and thereby encounter the truly sacred. It celebrates paradox and the wisdom of nonattachment.

JIM MAY was born in Spring Grove, Illinois, where his ancestors first settled in the 1840s. Raised in this small German-Catholic farming community, his stories resonate with the rural voices of the Illinois prairie. His relatives spent time "visiting" and telling stories as an integral part of daily life—a means of weaving the social fabric of the community. As an Emmy award-winning and world-traveling freelance storyteller and author, he seeks to reestablish direct person-to-person storytelling as an art form ideal not only for entertainment but for the grounding and healing that is needed in complex, modern times.

NARAS PHOTO

THE RUBY

The old man had slept the night at the edge of the village. He awakened at his usual time, just before sunrise, as a warm wind moved over the land, gathering up faint aromas that sweetened the air: a small garden here, a tiny blossom there, the pungent whisper-memory of a dying water hole.

He sat up, looked to the east where the sky was beginning to lighten, and began his morning devotions, starting the day with prayer as he had done almost every day of his life. It was during these prayers that the sound of hurried footsteps greeted his ears, and then a voice behind him: "Master, master, where is it?"

The old man turned slowly, and there standing behind him, was a young peasant, dressed in rags. The young man was excited, his chest heaving up and down, his eyes intense and piercing.

The old man studied the young man for a long moment. "What is it that you ask of me?"

The young man bowed slightly to his elder, seeming to calm himself a bit, and spoke: "I had a dream last night, and in my dream I came to the edge of the village and met a holy man. And now here you are. In my dream that holy man gave me a precious jewel."

"Ah," replied the old man as he reached down and retrieved from a clump of grass a ruby the size of a fist.

"You must mean this. I found it...I don't know where, but I have no use for it. You may have it."

With that the old man handed the ruby to the young peasant, a man whose hands had never held more than two copper coins at one time.

The young man took the ruby. He could not believe his good fortune. He held it up to the sun, his face awash in red shadow. He walked home slowly, holding the jewel in his hand, his arm outstretched in front of him. He could not take his eyes off of it.

Returning to his small cottage he placed the ruby on the table, pulled up the one chair that he owned, and sat all day admiring his treasure. He would turn the stone this way and that, slowly, reverently stroking this great gift over and over as the hours passed.

That night the young man had difficulty sleeping.

The next morning he was traveling to the fields, the ruby secure in his pocket, when he came upon the old man.

It is said that the young peasant approached the holy man, took the ruby out of his pocket, and gave it back.

"I do not want this. I want what you know that made it so easy to give it away."

A WORD FROM THE WISE

This is one of the most successful and powerful stories that I have ever come upon or told. It really tells itself and does not require any particular style other than perhaps simplicity. Make the images clear, and stay out of the way of the story.

I often tell it at the end of a program, sometimes adding the phrase, "May we be so wise," at the end. This addition is certainly not necessary and is actually as much concerned with the ceremony of ending the concert as with the story itself. This story is also an excellent focus for a lesson on the relative value of material and spiritual concerns.

Acknowledgments

"Against the Law OR Br'er Wolf Still in Trouble" appears by permission of James "Sparky" Rucker. Recorded versions appear on *Patchwork Tales: Stories from the Rucker Performance Archives* (Tremont Productions, TR005, 1996) and *Rainbow Tales, Too* (Rounder Kids, CD8034, 1997).

"B'Whale and B'Elephant" appears by permission of Derek Burrows.

"The Barking Mouse" appears by permission of Antonio Sacre.

"The Belly Button Monster" appears by permission of Olga Loya.

"The Bottle Imp" appears by permission of Bill Mooney.

"The Boy and the Devil" appears by permission of Pleasant DeSpain.

"The Changeling" appears by permission of Batt Burns.

"A Chelm Medley" appears by permission of Syd Lieberman.

"The Cherry Tree Buck" appears by permisson of Robin Moore. From *The Cherry Tree Buck and Other Stories,* available from Groundhog Press, Box 181, Springhouse, PA 19477 or on-line through www.robin-moore.com.

"The Dancing Fiddle" appears by permission of Dan Keding.

"Deer and Jaguar Share a House" appears by permission of Antonio Rocha.

"Dog Tails" appears by permission of Dovie Thomason.

"The Edge of the World" appears by permission of Rowena Walker.

"The Farmer's Fun-Loving Daughter" appears by permission of Taffy Thomas.

"Grandmother Spider Brings the Light" appears by permission of Sherry Norfolk.

"How Hare Drank Boiling Water and Married the Beautiful Pricess" is from *Why Goats Smell Bad and Other Stories from Benin* © 1998 by Raouf Mama. Reprinted by permission of the publisher, Linnet Books/The Shoe String Press, Inc.

"How the Rabbit Lost Its Tail" appears by permission of Len Cabral.

"Jean Sot and the Bull's Milk" appears by permission of J.J. Reneaux and August House Publishers, Inc. From *Cajun Folktales* © 1992 by J.J. Reneaux. Reprinted by permission of August House Publishers, Inc.

"Juan Bobo's Pig" appears by permission of Joseph Sobol.

"The Kiss of Evil" appears by permission of Loralee Cooley, with full knowledge and approval by TIME-LIFE Publications. The story from which this version is adapted appeared in the *Tales of Terror* volume of The Enchanted World series, published by TIME-LIFE in 1987.

"Little Frog and Centipede" appears by permission of Susan Klein.

"The Man Who Bought a Dream" appears by permission of Timmy Abell.

"Mary and the Seal" appears by permission of Duncan Williamson.

"The Nixie of the Pond" appears by permission of David Holt.

"One Wish" appears by permission of Liz Weir.

"Pine Trees for Sale!" appears by permission of Milbre Burch. From her audiocassette *The World Is the Storyteller's Village,* Kind Crone Productions, 43 Oakwood Drive, Chapel Hill, NC 27514. © 1994 by Milbre Burch.

"The Piper's Revenge" appears by permission of Billy Teare.

"The Praying Mantis" appears by permission of Deborah Joy Corey. From *YANKEE* magazine, Nov. 1991. Monthly Vol. 55, No. 11 (Dublin, New Hampshire: Yankee Publication Office).

"Redmond O'Hanlon and the Wee Fella" appears by permission of Maggi Kerr Peirce.

"The Ruby" appears by permission of Jim May.

"The Secret of the Animals" appears by permission of Michael Parent, Julien Olivier, and August House Publishers, Inc. From *Of Kings and Fools: Stories of the French Tradition in North America* © 1996 by Michael Parent and Julien Olivier.

"The Sky Is Falling" appears by permission of Jay Stailey.

"The Snake and the Frog" appears by permssion of Jon Spelman.

"The Story of Anniko" appears by permission of Charlotte Blake Alston.

"Sweet and Sour Berries" appears by permission of Linda Fang.

"Taen-awa" appears by permission of David Holt.

"The Tail of the Linani Beast" appears by permission of Margaret Read MacDonald.

"The Tale of Delgadina" appears by permission of Laura Simms.

"Tales of Aesop" appears by permission of Heather Forest. A musical collection of Aesop's fables retold in original poetry can be found on Ms. Forest's recording *The Animals Could Talk* (Little Rock: August House Audio, 1994). An extended collection of Aesop's fables and other concise folktales plots for students to retell can be found on Story Arts Online, an educational website for teachers and librarians about the use of storytelling in the classroom, www.storyarts.org.

"The Talking Dog" appears by permission of Doc McConnell.

"The Three Wishes" appears by permission of Martha Hamilton and Mitch Weiss and August House Publishers, Inc. From *Noodlehead Stories: World Tales Kids Can Read and Tell,* forthcoming in the fall of 2000.

"Tía Miseria" appears by permission of Harlynne Geisler.

"Tigertail Soup" appears by permission of Melinda Munger.

"Why Armadillos Are Funny" appears by permission of Barbara McBride-Smith.

"The Young and Dashing Princess" appears by permission of Beth Horner.

Index of stories by cultural source

South America

Index of stories by recommended audience

Middle School/Junior High:

High School:

Adults:

All Ages:

Family Audiences:

Ghost Story Setting:

Mixed Cultures or Immigrant Audiences: